SHIFT YOUR
PARADIGM

SHIFT YOUR PARADIGM

EMPOWER YOUR LIFE

& UNLOCK YOUR TRUE HIDDEN POTENTIAL

DIONIS J. RODRIGUEZ

NEW DEGREE PRESS

SHIFT YOUR PARADIGM
Empower Your Life
& Unlock Your True Hidden Potential

ISBN   978-1-63730-675-8 *Paperback*
          978-1-63730-764-9 *Kindle Ebook*
          979-8-88504-100-3 *Ebook*

For Nathaniel and Ariela

Contents

"Do not go where the path may lead, go instead where there is no path and leave a trail."

—RALPH WALDO EMERSON

Introduction

———

I've had an incredibly successful life. I was born at the bottom of society in a poor village in the Dominican Republic, but my parents' decision to immigrate to the United States created amazing opportunities for me. A combination of hard work, resilience, and excellent teachers and mentors allowed me to transform my life via education. After graduating from Cornell University and Harvard Business School (HBS), I achieved great career success, working for institutions like AIG and other multi-billion-dollar organizations. I climbed the corporate ladder and was unstoppable in all of my endeavors.

In 2013, four years after I founded and successfully led the Harvard Business School Real Estate Alumni Association, the school's newly appointed executive director of Alumni Affairs asked me to step down from my role as president of the volunteer organization I'd thrown my soul into. This blow came out of nowhere, leaving me feeling deeply betrayed by an institution I loved. I felt like a failure.

For the first time in my life, my motivation, focus, and drive to succeed were negatively impacted. My paradigm shifted, and I felt like a sailboat without a mast in a vast sea, unable to move in the direction I wanted.

I was powerless.

So I started to research motivation, self-awareness, and related topics in a desperate attempt to get my power and my life back. I searched deep within myself, looking for that strength I'd used to overcome past obstacles. Before all of this, I'd grown from an impoverished immigrant into a Harvard Business School alum and successful businessman. I was incredibly powerful. Everything had seemed easy, and then a single obstacle changed my personal lens. Even worse, I didn't understand why I felt that way or what I could do about it.

As a result of this difficult experience, for the past several years I've studied how people overcome significant obstacles to find their definition of success. What I have learned from countless books, articles, courses, internal and external dialogues, and other research is that humans are controlled by their *paradigms*.

Our personal paradigms determine how we view, react to, and feel about life and the world. We develop our paradigms throughout our lives as we form a view of the world and interpret events in light of our general sense of ourselves (our consciousness and our being) relative to the world. Our personal paradigm is our philosophy of what progress through life is all about, and includes a definition of "who I am" at any point in time, what the world is like, and how "I" interact with it. Paradigms are essentially the internal mental infrastructure—or computer mainframe, if you will—from which we view life, create feelings, filter experiences, and make decisions.

The biggest complicating factor for all of us is that this is a subconscious function, controlled by past experiences and easily shifted by negative and positive emotions. Thanks to my mentors and teachers, I had powerful paradigms that helped me achieve my definition of success up until I "failed," otherwise this negative experience would have prevented me from reaching my goals. It did not matter whether I really failed or not, because my internal lens believed my feelings reflected reality, which then impacted my motivation, actions, and overall life perspective.

We are all slaves to our paradigms.

I never got an official straight answer from HBS as to why they asked me to step down, but I was able to piece together what others believed happened after several discussions with folks from within the school, as well as wealthy alumni who are major donors to the institution.

Apparently, I was the brown face of a club that represented the most successful real estate alumni network in the United States and globally. I was not the right "fit" for the job because I am a person of color and come from an impoverished background, whereas they were "elite"—the most powerful real estate network in the world. I should have suspected a possible issue when, a year earlier, an alum and major donor likely worth hundreds of millions of dollars, casually told me the club needed "new blood." Since I founded the club and we were adding tremendous value, I did not think much of his comment at the time.

Eventually, I was able to understand it was not my "failure" that led to HBS asking me to step down, but a combination of classism and, I feared, racism by a small group of wealthy alumni donors who wanted a more acceptable person to lead their exclusive club.

I had such an amazing experience at HBS and a supportive relationship with the past executive director that my paradigm did not allow for that possibility. How could the world's preeminent management institution have poor leadership in one of its departments? And how could this leader prioritize the biases of some alumni over the extensive, multi-year volunteer efforts of younger, diverse alumni seeking to add value to an institution making a difference in the world?

What message would this communicate to others?

As Friedrich Nietzsche said, "That which does not kill us makes us stronger." This experience shocked my life plan, introducing uncontrollable elements I didn't see coming. It led to internal struggles, feelings, and emotions I was not used to. It forced me to see the real me and have more empathy toward other people. Facing the obstacle head-on allowed me to look at life more holistically and redefine my definition of success, but more importantly, it revealed that I needed to focus more on the journey than on the destination—that is where all the magic happens.

I gained greater self-awareness as a result and attained the personal power to free myself from a debilitating paradigm. I decided my paradigm was my responsibility—I had to acknowledge it, learn from it, and cultivate it to access my full potential. Finally, it unleashed a tremendous amount of gratitude for all the people and institutions that have positively shaped my paradigm, including HBS. I now understand I am paying their good deeds forward, since there is a multiplier effect to their efforts and kindness.

Success is not a destination, but a long, unending personal journey with numerous obstacles to be conquered. And sometimes, the greatest obstacles lie within us. Your paradigm determines your ability to achieve success, have meaningful relationships, make a difference to society, and secure a fulfilling and happy life. It determines whether you are a good parent, a good leader, a good friend, or a good person. However, our education system, leadership institutions, and self-help books focus primarily on the external factors that lead to success, leaving a significant opportunity for personal and societal improvement.

I was better equipped in that category than most people, as I have a Bachelor of Science degree from Cornell University and a Master in Business Administration from Harvard Business School. Nonetheless, I was unprepared to face difficult internal obstacles. Based on my research, we all go through difficult life experiences we are unprepared to address, which can result in a state of powerlessness. Though I was initially looking to solve my own problem, I came to realize society as a whole benefits substantially if we all focus on improving our paradigms.

Feeling like a failure was an emotional sensor pointing to an unconscious, internal struggle. I had achieved my long-term definition of success by excelling academically and getting myself out of poverty, graduating from Harvard Business School, and starting my own business. I accomplished what no one in my family had ever achieved; however, I needed a new definition of success to work toward—a new mountain to climb—and facing this problem opened my eyes to this subconscious feeling. At the time, my job was deeply unsatisfying and I was getting purpose and meaning from my volunteer work with HBS! When it was taken away from me, it felt personal and created imbalance in my life. The resulting journey of self-discovery, coupled with working on my paradigm, allowed me to let go of the debilitating belief that HBS betrayed me. Instead, I became grateful for the opportunity to be transformed into a better version of me.

Most of us have significant limiting beliefs preventing us from achieving our definition of success or otherwise limit our potential. These limitations are embedded in our paradigms and could result from numerous areas, including but not limited to traumatic childhood events, difficult life experiences, negative societal paradigms (such as racial injustices), socioeconomic conditions, and distinctions that make us feel less worthy than others. To make matters worse, we do not have the requisite self-awareness to understand that these issues impact our daily lives. We operate mostly on autopilot.

According to Dr. Tasha Eurich, an organizational psychologist, executive coach, researcher, and *New York Times* best-selling author, 95 percent of people believe they are self-aware, when the reality is just 10 to 15 percent of the population actually is. Can you imagine what a complicated society this creates and how difficult this problem is for relationships? All of us are controlled by our paradigms, but most of us don't realize this.

As Eurich states in her *Harvard Business Review* article, "What Self-Awareness Really Is (And How to Cultivate It)", "Research suggests that when we see ourselves clearly, we are more confident and more creative. We make sounder decisions, build stronger relationships, and communicate more effectively. We're less likely to lie, cheat, and steal. We are better workers who get more promotions. And we're more-effective leaders with more satisfied employees and more profitable companies." This means even a nominal increase in self-awareness, say 1 percent, would have a significant impact on the advancement of society.

Imagine if we actually lived in a society where, instead of the majority of us incorrectly thinking we are self-aware, most of us worked proactively on our paradigms. We are witnessing the unfortunate signs of limited self-awareness all around us. We are controlled by uncultivated paradigms, or worse, by those with the ability to manipulate our perspectives and beliefs. Politicians spend more time trying to hold on to power and blaming the other side than on solving problems for constituents. And yet, we still elect them! Most employees are unsatisfied with their careers and lack meaning and purpose in their lives, but they do not take actions to improve the situation. We know we are destroying the environment and experiencing greater climate effects than in recorded history, but do not curb our ways. Sadly, most of us spend more time on social media than quality time with our children and loved ones, which will have catastrophic consequences on relationships and society. At the same time, we are witnessing the reduction of the middle class and greater economic disparities.

The solution is to proactively work on our paradigms to lead better personal and professional lives as well as add value to society.

I realize I have the power to effect real change based on my transformation from an impoverished immigrant to successful entrepreneur, but more so because of my self-awareness journey. I want to help people understand that regardless of their specific situation, they have this power, too.

You have an incredible amount of power regardless of your birth circumstances or current situation. Most of it goes untapped because you operate subconsciously and you don't realize how truly powerful you are. Your worldview and abilities are limited by your paradigm at any specific point in time. However, you can unleash a tremendous amount of power allowing you to maximize the impact on your career, your family, and society by choosing to proactively study, shape, and—if necessary—shift your paradigm to one of power.

There is high likelihood you lack personal power in one or more areas of your life based on your paradigm—we all do. If you want to unlock your hidden potential and access your definition of success, this book was written for you!

CHAPTER 1

Wake Up! Acknowledge and Understand Your Paradigm

——

"If you want small changes, work on your behavior. If you want quantum leap changes, work on your paradigm."

—STEPHEN COVEY

In the blockbuster *The Matrix* (1999), the protagonist, Neo, seeks the truth about life. His feelings of unease about the surrounding world eventually lead him to the famous movie moment—should he take the red pill or the blue pill? The red will give him the paradigm of truth, while blue leads back to blissful naïveté.

Which pill would you choose, if you knew your paradigm was equally limited?

Neo, of course, chose the red pill and literally woke up by being physically disconnected from a computer world, only to discover he had been in a dream state his entire life.

WAKE UP TO ACCESS TRANSFORMATIVE POWER

Shockingly, our reality is not too dissimilar to *The Matrix*. Most humans go through their existence reacting subconsciously, as if in a dream state, to the paradigm they are born into and/or form early on in life. Very few humans are truly and fully aware of their paradigms and the potent power they have. Their personal realities are not in tune with true reality.

The difference is that most of us are controlled not by machines, but by our inability to empower ourselves. We live on autopilot, guided by our subconscious and by an insufficiently evolved mental process, which, if left uncontrolled, will lead to undesired consequences and a state of powerlessness. As Nigel Nicholson discusses in his *Harvard Business Review* article, "*How Hardwired is Human Behavior,*" evolutionary psychologists believe homo sapiens still seek the traits that made survival possible when they emerged from the Savannah Plains 200,000 years ago. He states that "although human beings today inhabit a thoroughly modern world of space exploration and virtual realities, they do so with the ingrained mentality of Stone Age hunter-gatherers." This "blue pill" is a vulnerable state of existence, but it is not the only option.

You have the power to choose and impact your paradigm and create your definition of success.

You are in mental bondage for two primary reasons. You probably are not fully aware of the first, and think you know more about the second than you really do. First, you are *biologically hardwired to live most of your life in autopilot,* making subconscious decisions based on your personal, created reality (primarily guided by fear and insecurity), which is not fully in sync with the real world (true reality).

You are *a prisoner of your mind.*

Second, this hardwiring, coupled with the physical/social circumstances you are born into, creates a debilitating state of paralysis robbing you of your power by limiting your self-awareness. Thus, there are biological, evolutionary, and physical reasons humans lack power and live an unfulfilled life.

Each one of us can choose the "red pill" by *deciding* to proactively work to unleash the tremendous amount of power within us. That is the dangerous truth! We can truly understand reality and decide how to go proactively, purposefully, and powerfully through our journey in life, regardless of who you are, where you were born, or what your specific circumstances are. This book will provide you with a process to accomplish this.

You can literally achieve anything you set your mind to, but it will require action and effort on your part. I'm a living example. Thanks to my paradigm and my decisions/efforts to impact my circumstances, I transformed myself from an impoverished immigrant to a Harvard Business School alum and successful entrepreneur.

If I can do it, so can you. So can anyone!

You can use the power you already have at your fingertips, and that comes from your decision to increase your awareness and proactively manage your paradigm. We will discuss this in more depth later, but by "power," I am referring to the ability to positively influence your thinking process and your circumstances, those of your friends/family, and of society as a whole; to the ability to choose and follow through with life-changing decisions regardless of your circumstances, and to manifest your definition of success—the power to free yourself from mental slavery and overcome your circumstances.

THE TRUTH SHALL SET YOU FREE

Jim Baggott is a science writer and activist. He won the Royal Society of Chemistry's Marlow Medal for his contributions to scientific research in 1989. He attended the University of Manchester for his undergraduate studies and the University of Oxford for a Doctorate in Chemical Engineering. He left his post as a tenured professor at the University of Reading, England for a career at Shell International Petroleum, but after eleven years started a business consultancy and training center. If you research him, you will find that he keeps busy as a prolific writer bent toward ensuring that scientists operate in fact and reality. He's quite opinionated and doesn't hold back. If he were to be described using contemporary social media parlance, we would call him a "troll," because of his intentionally provocative writing. But his ideas and perspectives are fascinating, especially as they relate to human behavior!

In his 2005 book *Farewell to Reality: How Modern Physics Has Betrayed the Search for Scientific Truth,* he accuses theoretical physicists speaking about multiverses, super string theory, super symmetry, and other potentially revolutionary scientific theories as "abstracted, theoretical speculation without any kind of empirical foundation." He describes those theories as "not science" and considers them in the realm of "metaphysics." As a life-long science aficionado and a lover of theoretical physics in particular, I believe this is an extreme view which I do not agree with, but I respect his perspective.

During his 2019 Berlin TED Talk, *Coming to Terms with Your Personal Reality,* Baggott says *The Matrix* essentially portrays a theory that philosophers came up with centuries ago: *we are prisoners of our minds.* "What we take to be reality is, in fact, entirely created from a sum of all of our experiences throughout our entire lives, from infancy right up to this TED Talk." He believes, like I do, that each of us has a unique and personal reality completely distinct from anyone else's—a reality created by our paradigms.

He also believes this makes each person's reality quite vulnerable to the control of those willing and able to manipulate it. While my goal is to convince you that you are *choosing* to live powerlessly, on autopilot, in your own created reality, Baggott's aim is to warn you about the potential for you to be brainwashed by people that can manipulate how your brain works. His conclusion is both accurate and concerning, as you will learn below. Let's first assess the three main arguments of his logic and see how it relates to our paradigms.

If everyone has a unique reality personal to them, then over-all, reality is simply a construct, comprising the collective paradigms of humanity. This is an idea I came up with as well (many people have), so no argument from me here. Baggott's point, however, is that since this is the case, then humans must suffer from an *Illusion of Explanatory Depth*, a term coined in 2002 by Yale researchers Leonid Rozenblit and Frank Keil. In a course on human behavior for the University of Edinburgh, Keil defines the Illusion of Explanatory Depth as "the sense that one understands complex phenomena more deeply than one does."

Jim Baggott believes this means the societies we create are so complex that no single human brain can comprehend them. To a significant extent, we rely on the knowledge and contributions of a few members of society, but this happens subconsciously. We believe we understand much more about the world around us than we actually do. Rozenblit and Keil wrote about this in their paper *The Misunderstood Limits of Folk Science: An Illusion of Explanatory Depth*. Their data is compelling. This reminds me of Tasha Eurich's findings about people believing they are much more self-aware than they really are. Taking this theory into consideration, her findings may overstate the level of self-awareness in society.

Let's look at a quick example. We use cell phones all the time. Some of us are quite savvy with them. However, if asked about how they function, most of us would incorrectly think we know, though we would actually have limited knowledge if pressed to provide details. This is known as the "knowledge of attribution effect." The fact that we use them and have easy access to them makes us feel like we know more much about them than we really do. Cell phones are very complicated. Do you know they rely on quantum mechanics to function, as well as the theory of the photoelectric effect, for which Albert Einstein won the Nobel Prize in physics in 1921 (Nobel Prize, 2021)? We take for granted that we walk around with a seriously advanced piece of someone else's human ingenuity.

This is the case for all other human inventions or societal constructs as well. Basically, we don't know what we don't know. While we walk around over-confident about our knowledge, we also suffer from something called the "reach around effect." When people think they know a lot about something (say yourself), they are more likely to think they know a lot about something related (like your self-awareness or your paradigm).

The Illusion of Explanatory Depth is a concept that applies to our reality as well. Since we share reality with all other humans, we take for granted the fact that ours is personal. We do not fully consider how much we do not know about true reality (the collective reality of all humans), since fathoming it would be impossible. We experience reality as a general process and believe we all share it—that everyone has the same reality we experience. That is not the case. Every reality is personal and separate, distinct from every other person's paradigm. We cannot understand or share anybody else's reality unless they let us in by discussing their thoughts with us.

The second point has to do with how humans make decisions. In his best-selling book, *Thinking Fast and Slow*, psychologist and economist Daniel Kahneman, who won the Nobel Prize in economics in 2002, describes two ways to process information since the brain has two operating systems.

You can think of System One as your gut, intuition, or muscle memory. It works lightning fast. Its defining characteristic is that it is an unconscious, automatic, and effortless process. It works *without* self-awareness or control: "What you see is all there is." Its main role is to assess the situation and to deliver updates. *System One does 98 percent of all of our thinking!*

System Two, on the other hand, is slow. Its defining characteristic is that it is a deliberate, conscious, controlled mental process resulting in rational thinking. The process is logical and skeptical, and acts with self-awareness or control. Its role is to seek new/missing information and to make decisions. *System Two does* only *two percent of all of our thinking.*

Based on this process and the speed at which they operate, our System Two is a slave to our System One. System One sends information to System Two, and this data can then be converted into beliefs. But there is a problem with the process.

Kahneman concluded that System One makes us all completely irrational because it operates in autopilot, subconsciously.

The reason this system operates in autopilot most of the time has to do with our ancestral survival instincts. Humans make 35,000 decisions a day, and our brain has to triage them or it'll go haywire. Thus, most decisions are made rapidly by System One, so as not to stress the system and kill the host.

This means the majority of human decisions are based on System One shortcuts, which Kahneman calls a "heuristic." But these short cuts are often wrong! Kahneman believes the way we "build" heuristics is by reviewing the information immediately at hand. We then relate that information to our past experiences—sort of like muscle memory. Therefore, heuristics (or System One shortcuts) are strategies derived from previous experiences with similar problems.

We are essentially re-living our problems if we are operating on System One, and we all do this 98 percent of the time!

Since the speed of getting that information for System One matters, we also overvalue information in the form of experiences our brain processes first. In this automatic process, first equals better. And this is the most astonishing piece of this puzzle. The by-product of heuristics is a reliance on the usage of our *cognitive biases.*

A cognitive bias is a systematic pattern of deviation from norm or rationality in judgment (Haselton, 2005). This means people create their own "subjective reality" from their perception of an input at hand. An individual's construction of reality, not the objective input, may dictate their behavior in the world. Thus, cognitive biases may sometimes lead to perceptual distortion, inaccurate judgment, illogical interpretations, or what is broadly called irrationality (Kahneman, 1972/ Baron, 2007/ Ariely, 2008). Our assessments about other people and situations could be made in an irrational fashion, reflecting not true reality, but our interpretation of it based on the mental process of hunter-gatherers.

Humans create their own personal reality from their perceptions, which are grounded mostly on past experiences and cognitive biases, and are the byproduct of an outdated mental process!

Baggott's third point is, based on the two points above, those who want to control us are already manipulating us. He points to a 2019 effort by Cambridge Analytica (working on behalf of politicians in a city in Germany) to spread misinformation on the basis of System One thinking to manipulate votes and how people felt about a specific issue. We will come back to this topic in later sections of the book, but suffice it to say his conclusions have been further confirmed since the filming of his TED Talk in 2019. The spread of misinformation by companies and individuals relying on strategies like those of Cambridge Analytica has placed the United States of America and democratic systems of government on life support. Many of us are being manipulated and we do not know it. Our System One processes have been hacked!

Baggott concludes his TED Talk by stating that "these System One manipulations threaten to change our personal reality. We go through life building these realities in our mind. It is very precious. It makes you who you are. It makes you unique. And what we have to do, not only as a society but also globally, is that we have to come to terms with the fact that we have to protect this reality [...]. The way to protect your personal reality is to be absolutely clear and aware of your vulnerability and then learn to be doubtful. Don't believe everything that you see."

I cannot argue with his conclusion, but I think the issue is much more severe than Jim Baggott describes. If we're mostly irrational beings with limited self-awareness—on autopilot, making decisions on the fly and based on past experiences using cognitive biases, living in our own personal reality—then our species is in grave peril at this point in our lifespan. This is complicated by the fact that *we do not have the ability to choose what to believe unless we first decide to become more self-aware and then practice challenging our perceptions.* Being effectively self-aware requires practice. Without that practice, we become paralyzed by not responding quickly to everyday events.

First, the Illusion of Explanatory Depth would make us assume and believe humanity is more advanced than it really is. All humans take credit for humanity's advancement, when the work has been done by a select few—the eighty/twenty rule, an aphorism asserting that 80 percent of outputs, in this case societal advancements, result from 20 percent of inputs (by humans) for any given event, likely applies here. It is no wonder we have launched numerous wars, have a crazy number of nuclear weapons globally at the fingertips of mad men, have enslaved each other throughout history, and are killing the planet. We are at a time in our civilization when we are sufficiently advanced to destroy our planet on the basis of one *irrational* decision by an *irrational* global leader.

Furthermore, as may already be happening without our knowledge, some powerful individuals can manipulate the System One processes of most of us to create unfair advantages granting them more power and control. This can be a government, the ultra-wealthy, the media, or any combination of these.

Baggott believes the solution is for us to be wary of the intent of those in power, but unfortunately, we cannot do that without self-awareness—most of us operate unconsciously. The prerequisite solution to this danger, to heed his advice, therefore, is for all of us to become responsible for our own self-awareness. We have to instruct our System Two processes to be responsible for the guidance and cultivation of our paradigms, so we can be conscious, self-aware, and operating in true reality. This is an area for which we cannot rely on the Illusion of Explanatory Depth, unless we want to be sheep at the slaughterhouse under the influence of a blissful "blue pill."

TAKING CONTROL OF MY PARADIGM

When I was twelve years old, I was offered a choice to meaningfully alter my reality. As a student at Nativity Mission Center—a free Jesuit middle school for at-risk immigrant youths in the "dangerous" Lower East Side of Manhattan—in the 1980s, I chose my path and accessed tremendous power. The alternative would have led me to a public high school with a 28 percent graduation rate.

The main purpose of my school was to offer excellent academics to poor immigrant students, ending the cycle of poverty through education. *I did not have to be poor like my parents and ancestors.* I could choose to do anything I wanted to do in life, but only if I succeeded academically and focused on developing my personal character.

While I did not feel we were well off, I didn't know we were poor until individuals I respected revealed that reality to me with my best interest in mind. Instead of accepting the circumstances I'd been born into, they offered me a chance to create my own destiny.

These renegade Catholic priests chose to help the poor, gaining my family's trust, and I gladly accepted their "red pill." To avoid their warnings of suffering, I prioritized my education above everything else, even relationships. They also equipped me with a strong sense of morality and ethics that proved to be invaluable. I graduated as valedictorian of Nativity Mission School (along with my friends David Duran and Kevin Rodriguez) and left with a dangerous and powerful paradigm: I could do anything I set my mind to, regardless of where I came from or any past experience.

My future was entirely up to me. I went on to attend Xavier High School in New York City on a scholarship from Nativity, followed by Cornell University for my undergraduate degree and Harvard Business School for a Master in Business Administration.

It worked for me. Proactively studying and trying to understand your paradigm can lead to meaningful self-awareness and great power with the ability to lead yourself and others to incredible heights. In fact, you can alter or shift your paradigm and create the future of your dreams. Just like I discovered for myself after feeling the same disturbing "something is wrong feeling" Neo felt, and then discovering the power was in my hands.

What is even more impressive is you can affect a societal paradigm shift and create value for humanity as a whole, like Martin Luther King, Jr. You can unlock the incredible amount of power you have to effect meaningful change for yourself, your business, and all of society.

All that is required is for you to decide to acknowledge and cultivate your paradigm to access power and transform your life.

THE FATHER OF PARADIGMS

Now that you understand your paradigm is essential for success and for the fate of humanity, let's talk specifically about what it is. The concept of a paradigm, as I am describing here, was first developed by the physicist and science historian Thomas Kuhn and described in his 1962 book, *The Structure of Scientific Revolutions.* He researched and wrote about how science develops over time and how scientific breakthroughs emerge.

Kuhn developed a scientific process for the advancement of science, over time. He first posed a theoretical question when he began to study Aristotle, realizing he did not understand the philosopher's scientific approach. To Kuhn, Aristotle's work seemed elementary and illogical, which he knew was definitely not the case for one of the greatest philosophers who ever lived and the first genuine scientist in history.

Another explanation had to exist. Kuhn later realized he did not understand Aristotle's *scientific* paradigm, which was completely different in 384 B.C. than it was in the 1960s.

Kuhn defined a scientific paradigm as "universally recognized scientific achievements that, for a time, provide model problems and solutions to a community of practitioners." He referred to this as "Normal Science." His five-step cycle first explains the absence of a paradigm, then how a paradigm is created by one or more scientists (normal science). As the scientific community uses the paradigm to solve issues, eventually one or more anomalies arise and the model experiences a "crisis," since it appears not to solve some new issues. The scientific community keeps working and eventually solves the anomalies by creating a new theory that correctly solves both past and new anomalies, leading to a paradigm shift and a new way of thinking.

The cycle continues to repeat itself as scientists work to better understand our world, benefiting all of society.

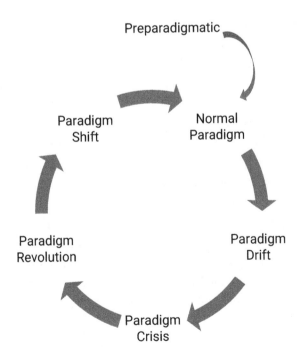

Let's take a high level look at how Kuhn's five-step science paradigm cycle theory works in the scientific arena prior to discussing how it is applicable to human behavior.

Thousands of years ago, early man had no concept about the shape of the world. It was not a relevant or necessary topic based on his daily experience. This was humanity's pre-paradigmatic state in relation to this topic. As civilization evolved, based on a combination of observation and theory, numerous ancient peoples—including the Egyptians, Mesopotamians, Greeks, Israelites, and others—theorized the world was flat, a paradigm that persisted for centuries or perhaps even millennia (Frankfort, 1949).

At the time, this belief provided all the solutions to the needs of these early "scientists," who relied on foot or beast for transportation. Many years later, the ancient Greeks—including Pythagoras, Anaxagoras, Aristotle and others—found anomalies in the theory based on additional advancements in society, leading to a model crisis. To solve this problem, they proposed the world was round, leading to a paradigm shift when they proved it. A new model paradigm was created for society. This discovery added tremendously to the advancements of humanity.

Kuhn's work has been applied to numerous other scientific fields, including sociology. The model demonstrates how paradigms are created and changed in communities of people. However, it also applies to human behavior as it reflects the process by which individual humans develop, expand, and change their internal perspectives.

My own experience and understanding of Kuhn's description of a paradigm led me to describe it for an individual as *the internal infrastructure of a person's personality, comprising the summation of all that person's experiences, interactions, thoughts, and emotions up to that point in time.* It is the internal machinery with which a person decides what to do and not to do, how to feel, what decisions to make, as well as the corresponding rationale for the same. Whereas Kuhn was referring to a community of scientists dealing with a theory or observation of the external world, our internal paradigms are guided by our own observations and accumulation of knowledge (through experiences, education, etc.), as well as interactions with others.

The key difference is that we are the only witness to our paradigms. To properly pilot them, we have to act like we are a community of scientists and constantly make observations about how we interpret life, testing them and arriving at important conclusions that may influence how we think. It must be a proactive, never-ending process if we are to make internal advances in the way that scientific communities move our society forward. And we must have vulnerable discussions with our friends and loved ones to allow other inputs to impact how we view the world. Relationships are key to your paradigm cultivation as, together with your experiences and thinking, they comprise a community of scientists.

It sounds simple, but the process is normally chaotic, complicated, and long. A scientific paradigm is comprised of several factors, including a sense of which theoretical components are foundational and least subject to doubt, a sense of the specific methods for testing theoretical advances, and an overall sense of what the highest priority tasks are for scientists to pursue within the paradigm. Because any one piece of empirical evidence is generally not sufficient to force a paradigm change, the challenge is knowing when to dismiss a sample of reality as inaccurate and when to follow up to see if the paradigm needs to change. The process is continuous and proactive and can involve significant trial and error.

As Kuhn observed, people are generally over-committed to their paradigm and hence not as accepting of empirical challenges as might be ideal. This is the case for scientific and personal paradigms. The point is that change and advancement are both methodical and transformational. They solve new challenges, but they become embedded in the current way of thinking for individuals or communities of scientists. Thus, a paradigm shift is revolutionary for both human behavior and the science community.

As emotional beings, our feelings play a major role in how we see the world and we act irrationally in light of our attachment to other people, ideas, or past traumatic experiences. This means changing our personal paradigms requires meaningful self-awareness and significant effort, which is the reason it can unlock so much of our potential. It offers a superior, enhanced way of seeing the world—like having poor eyesight and getting an updated prescription that restores adequate vision. However, our paradigms function whether we acknowledge them or not, being a crucial survival and advancement mechanism for the human species. Just as some civilizations and empires advanced faster than others, not guiding our paradigms is a major competitive disadvantage placing us at the mercy of those with sufficient self-awareness to focus on theirs.

Cultivating your paradigm is like deciding to create a map when you chose to go to a new destination. It may take a while, and roads and conditions change. You may have to turn back and double up a few times, but if you continue driving, you will get there eventually. You can choose to enjoy the scenery and find shortcuts for your next journey—cultivating your paradigm is an involved, proactive process. On the other hand, choosing no map to guide your life is like covering your eyes and trying to get somewhere, without really knowing where you want to go. It will be a dark, bumpy, and frustrating ride. Since you don't know the destination, any place will do. You will get stuck in numerous places thinking you arrived somewhere (or perhaps you are trapped), without ever getting to where you could have gone if you had decided on a specific destination in the first place. Imagine what the world would be like if we still believed it was flat, having chosen not to study our environment! That would be the equivalent to ignoring your paradigm.

Deciding to attend Nativity Mission School and proactively choosing to improve my situation was the turning point in my life. It sparked a new way of thinking for me, and it marked the point in time when I am confident my professional and academic career improved relative to my siblings, cousins, and other friends from the neighborhood. One single decision, which I stuck with for decades, powerfully transformed my life journey. This was a paradigm shift for me and it paid off.

Why not decide to cultivate your paradigm and reap the benefits of a more fulfilling life?

As Kuhn's definition of a paradigm suggests, paradigms can expand and shift, providing a greater and more holistic view of reality. Our paradigms determine how we view, filter, and interact with the world inside and outside of our mind. We typically refer to our paradigms as our mindset, point of view, perspective, or lens, but I feel those descriptors are outward-facing and do not describe internal characteristics of our being which allow us to interpret and therefore react to the world.

Our paradigms allow us to see the world in a specific way. Our experiences and interactions determine the way we see and interpret the world, as well as how we feel about it and ourselves. We all have internal algorithms—which Kuhn called models—by which we see and interpret life. We are effectively controlled by our paradigms, but they are not something we can touch and feel, so we don't spend much time talking about these abstract aspects of our human engineering. This lack of acknowledgment and focus is problematic.

We don't normally use them as a tool for our advancement or to empower ourselves. On the other hand, if you look at any successful business, you will see the inner workings of that business are studied, well understood, and proactively guided and shifted by senior members of the organization to maximize success.

Business strategy, the equivalent of working on our paradigms, is the most important factor of success in leading organizations. Business strategy is a constant discussion and is never permanent, since competition is fierce. It changes based on the marketplaces and the actions of competitors, capitalizing on innovations and new opportunities. I believe this proactive approach to dealing with their strategies—or their ability to impact the world—gives some companies extraordinary success. The same is true for our paradigms.

THE CREATION OF PARADIGMS

Helen Keller offers us a glimpse as to how paradigms are created. Helen was a happy child, but tragically, at nineteen months old, she contracted an unknown illness described by doctors as "an acute congestion of the stomach and the brain" that left her both deaf and blind ("Ask Keller," 2005). As she recalled in her autobiography, her existence was like being "at sea in a dense fog" (*The Attic*, 2018). At such a young age, she did not have much of a vocabulary, and the inability to see or hear turned her world into darkness. Without language, she could not properly communicate with herself or the outside world. Furthermore, the inability to see or hear meant she could not fully experience the world.

As was typically done at The Perkins School for The Blind, Anne Sullivan tried to teach Helen to communicate by spelling words into her hand. For example, with her own fingers, she spelled "d-o-l-l" on Helen's palm to give a name to the gift she brought her new student. After numerous attempts, Helen began imitating Sullivan's hand gestures. "I did not know that I was spelling a word or even that words existed," Keller wrote in her autobiography. "I was simply making my fingers go in monkey-like imitation" (*The Attic*, 2019).

When Sullivan allowed water to run over Helen's hand while spelling its name on her palm, her entire world came into existence: "I stood still, my whole attention fixed upon the motions of her fingers. Suddenly I felt a misty consciousness as of something forgotten—a thrill of returning thought; and somehow the mystery of language was revealed to me. I knew then that w-a-t-e-r meant the wonderful cool something that was flowing over my hand. The living word awakened my soul, gave it light, hope, set it free" (*The Attic*, 2018).

Words, language, and understanding were the doorway to her life's paradigms, and Helen, after exhaustive knocking, was able to walk through that door and access human's most basic, and likely most critical infrastructure—communication. Immediately after, Keller nearly wore out Sullivan by demanding the names of all the other familiar objects in her new world. Helen went from pre-paradigmatic to a fully-created paradigm and was able to interpret and interact with the world and with herself.

As a result of that paradigm shift, Helen Keller did not just conquer her challenges—she destroyed them by reaching achievements very few people could. She wrote fourteen books, was the first blind person to graduate from college (and Radcliff College, no less), and traveled the world, becoming the leading activist for people with her affliction.

RED OR BLUE PILL?

Helen had a more distinct journey to accessing her paradigm than most of us experience, which may be the reason it unleashed an incredible amount of power for her via meaningful self-awareness. For those of us who can see, hear, and speak without the obstacles Helen experienced, the importance of those gifts is normally taken for granted. We forget their power in helping us achieve desired success and find our purpose. But to Helen, who lived in darkness for many years, even her limited communication ability opened her eyes to the entire world and made her incredibly powerful and unstoppable. Likely because she had no choice due to her specific situation, Helen was very aware of her paradigm, and this awareness was tremendously empowering to her.

This is not naturally the case for us. We must opt in!

Unlike Helen, most of us do not have recollection or awareness of how our paradigms were formed. We don't have a strong recollection of how dark our world was like she did, keeping us connected to our paradigm. Like computer programs running in the background allow machines to function properly, we don't even notice our paradigms. We ignore them. We live in our personal realities and generally allow System One thinking to control our actions and our entire lives. The mind has an ingenious design, and we can more actively understand how we function to access more knowledge and power over ourselves.

Do you commit to working on your paradigm to access power and transform your life?

Principle 1: Commit to working on your paradigm by being aware of it and starting a life-long journey of self-discovery. It will not be easy, but it will make life more meaningful and allow you to access more personal power.

Say it to make it real:

"I now have knowledge of how important my paradigm is to access power and live a fulfilling life. I commit to working on my paradigm. Right now, I am embarking on a long-term, never-ending journey of self-discovery to cultivate my paradigm."

CHAPTER 2

Experiences and Relationships Expand Our Paradigm

———

"Paradigms power perceptions.
Perceptions power emotions."

—WILLIAM P. YOUNG

In October 2004, our class speaker, Warren Buffet (the billionaire genius investor) told 900 of us recently accepted students we were all winners in the "birth lottery." He said that by our place of birth, we had entered and grown up in a world with enormous advantages over the planet's six billion other inhabitants.

He didn't say this because we were born with the ability to attend such an esteemed institution—he himself was rejected by Harvard Business School and my odds were close to zero at birth. He said it because we were born in the United States of America—the land of opportunity.

I don't doubt that coming to the US opened doors with great opportunities for me. Warren Buffet was most definitely right in that respect. I am extremely grateful my parents sacrificed everything to give us a better life in this promising nation.

Where you are born and raised has a substantial impact on your paradigm. Mine was meaningfully shaped by the United States, and more specifically, New York City.

However, we should all be even more grateful for another less likely and more miraculous voyage, one we have all experienced. It's too bad we don't remember it—because regardless of who you are, where you were born, or into what circumstances, birth is the culmination of an incredibly competitive, dangerous, and highly unlikely journey.

According to Dr. Ali Benazir, a happiness engineer and behavioral change therapist with an undergraduate degree from Harvard College, an M.D. from UC San Diego School of Medicine, and an M.Phil. from Cambridge University, the chances of you being born as you are is one in 400 trillion, or 0.00000000000002 (Spector, 2021). As a past McKinsey & Co consultant, he is well versed in analytics. His calculations include the odds of your parents meeting, staying together, and having children, among numerous other factors.

The most interesting part of the journey, though, is when you start to become you, which occurs during the reproductive stage. A female has about 100,000 eggs in her lifetime. A male has approximately four trillion sperm cells. A single reproductive cycle involves one female egg and approximately 250 million sperm cells to succeed. Only one of these 250 million cells will be the fastest traveler and successfully fertilize the egg.

You were the winner of a competition against 250 million competitors!

Your birth journey will likely be your hardest and most challenging accomplishment ever! Your birth circumstances or current challenges are nothing compared to what you have already achieved by the time of your birth. You will also never face fiercer competition. You don't remember it, but now that you have some awareness of it, it's important you acknowledge how incredibly powerful you are at your core.

You are a born winner.

You also won the lottery in another way. The Sage of Omaha, Warren Buffet, was right. If you were born in a western society or one with sufficient rights and freedoms, with the ability to transform your situation through your efforts and actions, you are better off than most of the planet. Let's see what my father did after a traumatic experience when he chose to change his paradigm, a decision that transformed my life.

MY FATHER'S POWERFUL PARADIGM SHIFT

In 1978, when my sister Rosanna (Sania) was about three years old and our family was still in the Dominican Republic, she contracted diphtheria, a bacterial infection that can lead to difficulty breathing, heart failure, paralysis, and even death. My father, who did not own a pair of shoes until he was seventeen years old, was a taxi driver and would come home daily before noon to give my mother $1.50 so she could buy groceries and cook lunch and dinner for the family. While I don't remember ever being hungry or unfed, food security was a daily struggle.

With my sister ill at the hospital, my father was told a surgery to save her life would cost 300 Dominican pesos. Unlike the US, Dominican doctors would not perform the surgery until the funds were paid in full. My father did not have that kind of money. He went to his friends and family members seeking a loan to save his daughter's life.

The majority of people in our little rural village were just like us, with no money, and for the most part dependent on subsistence farming and other entrepreneurial efforts. "My daughter is going to die," he kept saying to himself, as a motivation to unearth every possible option to save her life.

The situation was dire, and he didn't have much time. My older brother, Pedro, and I stayed with my grandfather, while my mom did not leave the hospital for even a second, probably not eating a bite of food while she waited there. I was only four years old at the time and, while I recall staying with my grandpa, I could not understand that the situation was so sensitive.

My father's refusal to fail and his honorable reputation (and lender's trust in his "word") were the only valuables he could exchange for the loans. Miraculously, he secured several smaller loans that totaled the required amount to save my sister's life. These loans were almost impossible for him to repay. He had to borrow more to repay maturing loans several times, until he was able to extricate himself from this vicious cycle and repay them all. However, the experience of his daughter almost dying and subsequent hurdles traumatized him.

My father felt powerless and vowed to never, ever allow himself to be in a similar situation again. As was the case for everyone else in our town, life was difficult, but this was the straw that broke the camel's back, in his perspective. This experience was the catalyst for him deciding to immigrate to the United States of America in search of better economic opportunities for himself and his family.

If you've never given up your language, culture, family, and comfort zone to move to another country where you will be at the bottom of society as an impoverished, penniless immigrant, it would be difficult for you to comprehend the gravity and courage involved in such a decision. It comes from a paradigm of trauma, survival, love, unselfishness, and a powerful (and desperate) growth mindset manifested by a need for action. At the core, immigration is a deeply courageous, rational, and risky move!

What needs and goals in your life have led to rational, well-thought-out, risky, and uncomfortable decisions or actions that, in retrospect, shaped your life?

EXTERNAL FACTORS THAT INFLUENCE YOUR PARADIGMS

As we saw in the last chapter, we are born paradigm free. As was the case for Helen Keller, paradigms begin to develop very early on in life and continue to grow and change for the rest of our days. They are impacted by both our internal mental processes as well as by our external circumstances.

Let's explore some of the physical factors likely to have the most significant impact on us. Some of them happen early on in life and you do not have control over them, whereas others you can control or impact if you chose to do so.

As you read below, think holistically as to how different your paradigm would be if any of these factors had been different for you. This will help you have greater awareness of how they shape your thinking.

BIRTH LOCATION

Your birth location is important because it determines your language, culture, physical attributes (in most cases), and, more importantly, the structure of the local society, and thus, your perceived freedoms and opportunities. As an example, if you are born in a communist country, like North Korea, it would require you to escape the country to achieve the basic rights that other countries, such as Switzerland, offer. Can you imagine what life would have been like for Helen Keller in North Korea?

For leaders to stay in power, the paradigms of people in repressed regimes must be vastly limited. Expanded paradigms, as will be discussed later, inevitably lead to people fighting for their rights and for the creation of freer, fairer, and more advanced societies. The advancement of civilization depends on expanded, free paradigms.

Democratic societies allow and, in some situations, encourage free thinking and free paradigm formation. Free thinkers, such as Aristotle, Plato, Galileo Galilei, Isaac Newton, Albert Einstein, Mahatma Gandhi, Martin Luther King, Jr., and Leonardo DaVinci, among many others, have added meaningfully to the advancement of society. They have shaped our paradigms.

Good leaders encourage people to empower themselves. Dictators and power-hungry autocrats attempt to limit the paradigms of the populace. They prefer to control them and keep power for themselves. This characteristic can be seen in democratic societies en route to become authoritarian nations. Their leaders manipulate and brainwash them, taking away their power. Unfortunately, our subconscious mental processes make this easier than we can possibly fathom.

This happened in Germany during the rise of Adolf Hitler and is quite common in non-democratic societies. Some would argue the US is experiencing similar issues today as evidenced by leaders seeking to divide the people in an effort to keep power and control. True leaders unite and want everyone to access information and have voting rights. Power-hungry leaders divide and create misinformation to align those they can manipulate to their cause. Now that you're aware of System One thinking, watch out for politicians telling you how to think about education, the media and other paradigm-expanding options. An attempt to limit information or tell you how to think or feel is a bad sign.

YOUR PARENTS AND UPBRINGING

We normally spend the first eighteen years of our lives with parents, starting from a pre-paradigmatic state at birth until we are young adults. Our paradigms are meaningfully shaped during this time period. We have the ability to model after our parents and have extensive experiences and interactions with them, family members, fellow students, and friends.

Parents have the most significant impact on a person's life and mindset. They determine social status, religion, birth locations, and race, and influence relationships, education, and other important characteristics in the development or expansion of paradigms.

They also pass their prejudices, biases, judgments, and opinions to us, a form of inadvertent indoctrination that may create insecurities, fears, and limiting beliefs.

SCHOOLING AND EDUCATION

Education expands the paradigms of students and, by so doing, changes the world. Schools are basically human growth labs exposing us to the most important aspects of life at the most critical period of our mental growth. We learn how to read, write, socialize, communicate, and interact with others in school. We are exposed to and engaged in sports and other competitive games via school programs, and of course we are taught history, science, government, and the inner workings of society.

We're also exposed to a diverse set of people, perspectives, and ideas that can meaningfully expand our thinking and mind frames. Education is critical to the advancement of society and human behavior. As top colleges and universities have discovered, greater racial and socioeconomic diversity create higher-performing students.

Though no formal education (except, perhaps, Jesuit education, of which I am a product) discusses the existence or creation of your paradigm and how your life lenses are shaped in the way I am describing in this book, school is a critical trial-and-error approach to how you learn—the physical manifestation of a heuristic, in a sense. Many of us see school as a way to prepare students for careers and jobs as adults, but they are much more important.

Education is the catalyst for the advancement of the individual, society, and democracy. Countries like the US in large part owe their growth and success to its education systems. As a result, the job of a teacher, after parents, is the most important career. Parents and teachers are our guides, life coaches, and role models at the most crucial times of our lives, when our paradigms are developing, and we are making choices that will impact us forever.

SOCIOECONOMIC STATUS

The belief that one's family is either advantaged or disadvantaged relative to others has a significant impact on a person's paradigm. If you are poor, you will witness others having better homes, cars, and other material possessions than you, as well as access to better services and even superior treatment from others based on their wealth. These experiences create emotions that will empower or hold you back.

In the capitalistic, material world we live in, it is natural then that poor people feel less worthy while the wealthy act superior to those of lower standing in society. The fact that a person can have greater or lesser value than another based on material possessions is of course preposterous. It is a human construct created by those with power (or by the insecurities of those without it), a way for the fragile human ego to feel worthy of itself. It also has a major impact on our paradigms and how society functions.

If a person from a poor family believes this nonsense, they create limiting beliefs impacting their power and ability to manifest their idea of success. If we look back at history and list the greatest humans who ever lived, using a metric of people that added value to society, we will come up with names such as Jesus Christ, Aristotle, Mahatma Gandhi, Nelson Mandela, Albert Einstein, Isaac Newton, Marie Curie, and other key figures who were not wealthy and significantly advanced our society.

From the true perspective that humans are all equal, what characteristics of an individual would you value most?

Looking at other humans and society from a paradigm of truth, and not allowing our lens to be controlled by our biases and how society tells us to view reality, are crucial.

RACE

The simple fact of having different skin color has fundamental societal and paradigmatic consequences. The reality is that according to the accepted theory of human evolution, all modern humans, including *you*, share a common ancestor who lived around 200,000 years ago in Africa. As Richard A. Strum, a professor at the University of Queensland, Australia, said in his article, "*A Golden Age of Human Pigmentation Genetics*" for the *Trends in Genetics Journal*, there is a direct correlation between the geographic distribution of ultraviolet radiation and skin color.

His research reveals areas closer to the equator receive higher amounts of ultraviolet radiation. As a result, people that live there have darker skin color. This would explain why indigenous peoples from Africa, Caribbean, Mexico, and other areas have darker skin tones, whereas Europeans and people far away from the equators don't.

Thus, the sun and where your ancestors have lived determine the color of your skin (and your eyes and other features). Another accepted fact of human evolution is that we were nomadic people who originated in or near Africa. Thus, your ancestors were African and had dark skin color.

You are African, genetically speaking. We *all are*, though we have developed unique, regional cultural identities.

How does that fact make you feel as you read it?

You likely have numerous biases as part of your paradigm that will resist this thinking and possibly make you (subconsciously) upset at me for even suggesting it, if you are not African or African American. These are your System One processes at work. We will discuss cognitive biases below and in other chapters.

DISABILITY

As is the case with socioeconomic concerns, the main problem with disabilities are not the disabilities themselves, but the distinctions drawn by the individuals and society as they compare people with and without these conditions. Looking at it from society's paradigm, one would think someone with a disability has less worth. This is a human construct based on cognitive biases.

If all of society was born with the same disability, it would not be a limiting condition at all in the eyes of society. From that perspective, neither society nor an individual should limit their paradigms based on a disability (or for any reason!).

Disabilities (better described as Different Abilities) can result in having to do things differently than society, but as Helen Keller, Greta Thunberg, Stephen Hawking, Albert Einstein, Andrea Bocelli, and many exceptional people have shown us, they can also be extremely empowering, if viewed from the right lens. View your disabilities from a paradigm of power and do not put on the lenses that society may want to offer you to perceive yourself and your condition.

All of us, disabled or not, can become disabled by wearing society's lenses, which are clouded by our biases.

PAST TRAUMATIC EXPERIENCES

Your mindset can be meaningfully impacted by traumatic events, such as physical or mental abuse, a car accident, or any experience resulting in extreme fear, pain, or disability. Traumatic experiences can affect a person's beliefs about themselves and their expectations for the future.

Trauma is often manifested in the reliving of negative events that occurred at a time when one felt powerless. As that person grows, gains power and confidence, and learns their value, they will be unable to overcome the experience and heal without meaningful effort.

Trauma can lead to hopelessness and limited expectations about ourselves or life. It can create irrational fears that life will end abruptly or early, or anticipation that normal life events won't occur. It can also be the platform for the creation of a stronger and more complete paradigm, if the person is able to transform the negative experience into a powerful and more informed perspective, as was the case for Greta Thunberg, who we will discuss in a later chapter.

GENDER

Since the beginning of time, men and women have had different roles in society shaping their perceptions, paradigms, and realities. Imagine you are a woman in Saudi Arabia versus a man in the United States today. Which paradigm could access more power? Why is that still the case in a modern world?

Your gender has a major impact on your mindset, either positively or negatively, especially if your expression of your gender is aligned or misaligned with your cultural expectations.

We all fundamentally understand the impact gender has on how we perceive life. The main issue is that we view reality only from our own perspective. As an example, we know women are generally paid less on average compared to men, and that it's more difficult for them to advance in most careers. They also typically have more family and child-rearing responsibilities.

Why do men—sons, brothers, and fathers of women—create and allow this injustice? These paradigms are created from birth for both genders and are difficult to change. They have a significant impact on how we see both the world and ourselves. For the most part, we accept and operate from the "normal paradigm" that was established long ago. We accept the roles passed down to us for millennia.

The honest truth is, in most societies (probably all of them), men benefit from the differences in power, so don't expect a radical change any time soon—at least not without a hard-fought battle. Women will have to work on, expand, and shift their paradigms to access more power than society allows them to perceive.

My friend and Cornell classmate, Leighann Sullivan, PhD, a professor of biology and chemistry, does not think women will get there in small increments as I am suggesting above. She believes it'll take a major societal upset for women to attain true power with men. Based on how difficult it is to change paradigms, as we learned in the last chapter, she is probably right.

RELATIONSHIPS

Relationships are the most powerful force guiding our paradigms. They are the arena where the game of life is played. They are the source of empowerment or destruction of your paradigm. They provide meaning or hopelessness. Marriage, friendships, and other healthy relationships have been scientifically correlated to long life, better health, and happiness. We have also seen that isolation is destructive to our paradigms, our meaning, and our purpose. Furthermore, limiting beliefs and stuck paradigms are likely created based on relationships. There is direct connection between your relationships and your mental and physical well-being.

On one side, you have a fearless gladiator (you); on the other side, you have a shape-shifting and deceptively intelligent combatant that controls your feelings, actions, and decisions (your relationships). If you do not know how to battle (limited self-awareness, uncultivated paradigm, etc.), you will be lost in the fight. But if you do, your collaboration will be a magnificent source of power adding value to the world. Relationships are a power magnifier or power destroyer. You can plug into them for power or they can lead you to a world of unproductive and never-ending drama.

You have to also keep in mind that biases and other issues that impact your paradigm are created from interactions with other humans and society.

RELIGION

Looking back at history, the story of humanity, and the advancement of civilization, substantial evidence demonstrates that faith in a higher power is a positive contributor to our outlook on life. According to Paul S. Mueller, MD, David J. Plevak, MD, and Teresa A. Rummans, MD in their article *"Religious Involvement, Spirituality, and Medicine: Implications for Clinical Practice,"* for the Mayo Clinic Proceedings, religious involvement and spirituality are associated with better health outcomes, including greater longevity, coping skills, and health-related quality of life (even during terminal illness), as well as less anxiety, depression, and suicide. Several studies have shown addressing the spiritual needs of the patient may enhance recovery from illness.

Fundamentally, faith shows us how to think about the world and our role in it, which is the basis for our paradigms. Characteristics associated with religious beliefs, such as love, hope, optimism, morality, connectedness, trust, and purpose, increase or are related to good mental health. Empathy, forgiveness, selflessness, and gratefulness are also qualities strongly associated with individuals who are spiritual and religious. Practicing these qualities is thought to be associated with decreased stress, increased resiliency and a positive life outlook.

Religious people have a strong internal sense of control, likely as a result of the required introspection and reflection to be faithful. Dr. Harold Koenig of Duke University contends that as people pray and ask God for guidance, they feel a sense of control over their own situation, helping them cope with depression and anxiety.

Religion also creates a strong, connected community of people who share the same beliefs. Because religion is typically a form of positive psychology, guiding moral development in humans, it has a strong impact on the creation of a principle-centered paradigm, which we will discuss in a later chapter.

Acknowledging that atrocities have occurred numerous times throughout history in the name of religion is also important; however, the fact that humans use religion or other reasons in search of self-gain and power is no surprise, and has nothing to do with spirituality, or the belief in or benefits of a god-centric perspective.

COGNITIVE BIASES AND THE ENORMOUS SEDUCTION OF NOW

Paradigms are at the intersection or your internal self and the world around you. We live in a complicated world with billions of other humans and together we create human civilization. System One thinking shows we are predisposed to live in the now and to make irrational choices that prioritize the present over the future. This sounds like a simple fact about our behavior, but it has massive implications for your life and for civilization as a whole.

Cognitive biases are an essential System One mental process but they force us to be on autopilot, as if in a dream state. They were responsible for allowing our species to have survived throughout history (survival of the fittest), but they also take away our power by eliminating rational choice in most situations. These repeating biases are deeply ingrained in our personal reality and are a core component of our paradigms.

The great book *Sapiens: A Brief History of Humankind*, by Yuval Noah Harari, demonstrates why heuristic shortcuts are representative of a time when humans were less evolved. Our society has changed significantly—from being nomadic hunter-gatherers and relying mostly on short term System One thinking for survival, to today, where, as non-nomadic peoples, we should rely more on System Two thinking.

We are now an established species controlling the planet. But we are still genetically predisposed to Stone Age hunter-gatherer thinking. Our mental evolution has not caught up to our modern way of life. Our mental processes, to a significant extent, still function as was required for a hunter-gatherer way of life.

FUTURE SELF-CONTINUITY AND HYPERBOLIC DISCOUNTING

Dozens of cognitive biases exist and many more will likely be discovered. Behavioral economics is a young and insufficiently understood scientific field gaining increasing popularity. Unlike classical economics, which assumes humans are rational, it takes what is a more realistic stance and starts with the assumption that humans are irrational.

The cognitive biases we are most concerned with in this chapter are "future self-continuity" and "hyperbolic discounting." They relate to how you interpret the world and make everyday decisions facilitating those interpretations, leading to specifically timed actions and emotions.

The psychological concept of "future self-continuity" is simple but has strong implications for your ability to manifest your definition of success. It states that the degree to which we feel connected to our future self in the present (insert a goal, such as "I want to be a CEO," if you are a student) dictates whether we ensure the well-being of that future self (Mohammad, 2020). In other words, strengthening our future self-continuity can lead to improvements in our decision-making, such that we can bypass System One thinking and create that future self.

When I was twelve years old and decided to transform myself via education, I saw my future self as the CEO of a company. Because I was able to honor my word for my decisions, I know in retrospect that I had strong future self-continuity. This was important because it kept me connected to my goals for many years. I did the planning, hard work, and prioritization to become my future self. I was extremely confident in my ability to do so.

If you don't have strong future self-continuity, then you will suffer the consequences and instead experience "hyperbolic discounting."

When my brother, Pedro, was about fourteen years old in the mid-1980s, he became passionate about computers. He asked my father for money to buy one. My father, who wanted to please his son but did not have a lot of money, told him, "I can give you $150 now, or you can wait a month or so and then I can give you $500, or the amount necessary so you can buy a full computer, with a screen and everything."

Pedro was impatient and took the $150, which he used to by a Commodore 16. This early personal computer consisted of only a keyboard connected to a TV set and could do basic functions. He was beyond happy, but I've always wondered about the potential changes to his life had he selected the more rational option. My brother is highly intelligent and extremely talented, so he could have been another Bill Gates or Michael Dell.

Research shows that what my brother did is quite common— people routinely give up significantly more valuable future items for in-the-moment satisfaction.

"Hyperbolic discounting" demonstrates that as the time it takes to receive a reward increases, the value we assign to that reward is "discounted." Intellectually, we know and can measure that this type of short-term gratification is not rational. If you eat that ice cream or that slice of pizza, you will suffer the consequences later. It's not the first time you do so, and you know that continuously giving in to your urges will have serious implications for how you look, what your friends will think of you, and your long-term health. But we give in to short-term gratification *all the time*. We overvalue short-term rewards to the detriment of achieving long-term goals.

The reverse problem also exists. Some people do not enjoy the opportunities of the present because they are only focused on the future. Self-awareness and balance are essential.

SO WHAT ARE THE IMPLICATIONS TO YOUR PARADIGM?

Cognitive biases are subconscious, transparent, and automatic aspects of our System One thinking processes. Think of the implications this has on your future and the creation of your personal reality and society. If you drew the short end of the stick for any of the external physical factors we discussed above, your future self-continuity is going to be routinely defeated by your hyperbolic discounting unless you activate System Two mental processes. What will this do to your paradigm if you don't?

If you are a female, and for all of history you have been defined in a less valuable way than a man, how can you overcome your hardwiring to ensure a strong continuity of self?

If you are African American, you are aware of the terrible injustices to people from your background, historically and in the present. You see it all the time. How easy or difficult would it be for you to have a strong continuity of self under these unfair conditions if, as a youth, your goal is to be a lawyer, doctor, or professor?

Have you ever experienced hyperbolic discounting in any area of your life?

As a society, are we experiencing "hyperbolic discounting" in regards to climate change, politics, or other areas?

Behavioral economists assign monetary value to compare present and future to prove this point, but I think our emotions play a bigger role than material possessions. I think fear in the present can put a monkey wrench into any future plans. Our emotions make us highly irrational. Our irrationality could be easily created by an emotional or sensorial response that feels more urgent compared to a rational and more valuable longer-term response that may never materialize.

To overcome System One Thinking, we have to engage System Two mental processes and create rational short- and long-term goals we revisit frequently. You may give in to your urges, but stay focused on the task at hand, knowing System One processes are responsible. You have to be persistent and unstoppable in the face of challenges; however, you now know the game and its rules. Like in a basketball game, you must be on the court, constantly playing; don't be a spectator in your own life! Yes, you will miss shots, have turnovers, and be out with injuries at times, but be relentless. Pass the ball and involve other players, and don't stop playing until the game is won and your goal is reached. If you play in this style, which is how I played my game, I guarantee you will succeed.

Principle 2: Create long-terms goals and focus on maintaining strong continuity of self. Be relentless. Don't stop playing until you win the game!

CHAPTER 3

Stuck Paradigms and Limiting Beliefs

———

"Knowing yourself is the beginning of all wisdom."

—ARISTOTLE

The inability or unwillingness to be vulnerable and express our genuine sentiments will create limiting beliefs, insecurities, and stuck paradigms holding us back. When we do this, we move in the opposite direction of self-awareness. We create a personal reality out of sync with true reality. We enter a subconscious realm of self-denial. Our mental processes do this automatically.

Vulnerability, conversation, and revealing our genuine feelings and thoughts to our friends and ourselves is a requirement for both understanding and expanding our paradigms. It sets us free by providing the proper contextual understanding of our internal issues or emotions and connecting us with true reality. It syncs our awareness of self with reality.

GOOD WILL HUNTING—THE INSECURE GENIUS

In the 1997 American drama film *Good Will Hunting*, the protagonist was abused by his foster parents as a child. Despite being a genius, he is not living up to his full potential. He is controlled by his insecurities. He could be a leading mathematician advancing society to new heights of understanding, but is a janitor at MIT instead, hiding from his talents and himself.

Will initially refuses to cooperate with his psychiatrist, Dr. Sean Maguire, with whom he has much in common. They both come from a blue-collar background, grew up in South Boston, love baseball and, sadly, were abused as children.

Like most of us, he has limited self-awareness and resists self-improvement. Dr. Maguire is patient, though, and Will begins to open up. He challenges Will to step outside his comfort zones. He asks him questions that probe deep into his subconscious and his past. Will begins to see how limited his paradigms are in certain matters, such as love and romance, when Dr. Maguire shares his own experiences genuinely, in a vulnerable and risky way. As they exchange stories, experiences, and secrets, their relationship strengthens. Will is able to be more vulnerable.

A few key scenes are climactic. Months after Will meets and falls in love with Skylar, a Harvard student about to leave for Stanford Medical School, she asks him to move to California with her. Will has not been honest with Skylar about his background. He has lied or left out aspects he believes are undesirable or unlovable. Perceiving an incredible risk to a real commitment with Skylar, he questions her sincerity about wanting him to accompany her. Subconsciously, he does not want to get hurt.

When Skylar questions what he is so afraid of, the impostor explodes, "You just want to have your little fling with the guy from the other side of town, then you're going to go off to Stanford, then you're going to marry some rich prick that your parents will approve of and just sit around with the other trust fund babies and talk about how you went slumming too once."

He finally shares his truth: he is an orphan and his father burned cigarettes on his back and stabbed him.

Will lacked self-love and blamed himself for what happened, which prevented him from opening up and loving others without fear. As a psychiatrist, and based on his personal experience, Dr. Maguire understood the significant obstacle created by the physical abuse Will suffered. He forces Will to honestly face, admit, and reflect on the abuse to allow him to be freed from his limiting beliefs.

FEAR IS YOUR GREATEST NEMESIS

Acknowledged or not, we all have fears that control us. The second you allow fear to enter your paradigm, System One takes over and makes it part of your personal reality. Fears create limiting beliefs about ourselves that, if unaddressed, will result in a stuck paradigm—a belief so central to our being it becomes fundamental to how we filter and interact with life. It imprisons us and limits our possibilities in relationships and life, as was the case with Will Hunting.

That's why understanding your paradigm can give you meaningful access to personal power, stronger relationships, and a greater ability to influence others and society. If you can become conscious of them and proactively face your fears, you will become unstoppable.

If you give in to fear, you will not reach your full potential.

Every single human being has experienced the sort of mental trauma leading to fears and negative limiting self-beliefs. There are no exceptions—we all have baggage created from one or more of the external factors we discussed in the last chapter.

As you think about *Good Will Hunting*, consider your own life and where you may have negative limiting beliefs, fear, hesitancy, or other aspects that have resulted in stuck paradigms. Where would Dr. Maguire probe to bring out and help you face and deal with a hurtful past? What personal paradigm could he share to help you become vulnerable enough to open your life to possibilities and help you uncover your definition of success?

Who is the Skylar of your life trying to get you to open up and expand your possibilities? Why do you resist?

In one way, shape, or form, we are all Will Hunting. We may not have a genius IQ, but we all have limiting beliefs disempowering our reality and holding us back. The only way to free ourselves is to face them.

"What you resist, persist!"

—CARL JUNG

VULNERABILITY DEFEATS FEAR AND
EXPANDS YOUR PARADIGM

Fears are like mice or cockroaches living inside your home. They survive by hiding, staying out of sight and feeding on your System One processes, your biases, and anything else they can ravage, all while you are not paying attention. They do not want to be exposed because they lose their ability to feed and control you. Fears can be deeply irrational. They are a sensor indicating something is wrong and needs attending.

Our most fundamental fear is human disconnection.

Helen Keller experienced how language was the way to her connection with Sullivan and the world outside of her head. Language is the way we can share ourselves and our paradigms and "connect" with others. We don't fully understand why, but an inability to truly connect with others is destructive to our paradigms and results in our being out of sync with true reality.

Brené Brown, a researcher, storyteller, and professor at the University of Houston, has done extensive research on fear and shame. Her book, *Daring Greatly: How the Courage to be Vulnerable Transforms the Way We Live, Love, Parent and Lead*, explores how embracing one's vulnerability and imperfection is necessary for achieving real engagement and social connection. She experienced a paradigm shift when she discovered the importance of vulnerability. Her research literally changed her life, resulting in her spending a year in therapy, as she described it, to be able to grasp and accept what she discovered—to make it part of her reality. Prior to her discovery, she was an introvert, but was forced to transform herself based on both her work and the success obtained because of it.

During a TEDx Houston event about expanding perception, Brown described vulnerability as "a piece of my research that fundamentally expanded my perception and really actually changed the way that I live and love and parent." She states that her research led her to an astounding conclusion. One that that she fiercely resisted because it was the opposite of what she believed—"to understand vulnerability, you have to understand human connection because connection is what gives us purpose and meaning." She discovered that shame and fear are the major barriers to establishing proper human connections (Brown, 2021).

"Research showed that shame, which is easily understood as the fear of disconnection—'is there something about me that if other people know it or see it, I won't be worthy of connection.' It is universal. We all have it. What underpins this shame, the feeling of I am not good enough, is excruciating vulnerability. In order for connection to happen, we have to allow ourselves to be seen, to really be seen."

By being seen, she means to express yourself so honestly in conversation so as to allow the other person "to see" inside your paradigm with full transparency. Though we all shy away from doing this, we don't have full awareness of how difficult it is to do. When was the last time you opened up to someone without holding back fears or information?

Brown's extensive research demonstrated that there are two types of people in the world.

A group she calls *wholehearted* are people with a sense of worthiness and a strong sense of love and belonging. These people *believe* they are worthy of love and belonging. They have the courage to be imperfect and the compassion to be kind to themselves first and then to others. They are authentic. Wholehearted people are willing to let go of who they want society to see them as, opting for being seeing as they truly are. Their personal reality is highly in tune with true reality based on their authenticity (Brown, 2021).

Fundamentally, wholehearted people fully embrace vulnerability. They are not necessarily comfortable in this space, per se (not many of us are), but they have the self-awareness to understand it is essential to human connection and authenticity. They operate from a rational System Two mental process.

While she does not talk about the sizes of the two groups, it is evident she believes the second group, which does not embrace vulnerability, is massive. She insinuates the main problems of society exist because this second group avoids vulnerability. They are numbing themselves to love, caring, connection, and belonging because they give in to shame and fear.

She describes an obese society that is extremely materialistic and doesn't care for their fellow humans, a world full of people self-focused and disconnected from each other. They are fiercely trying to connect to each other by avoiding their shame and fear, so the opposite happens. They don't understand the formula or perhaps they resist it subconsciously, in the same way Brown did when she discovered it and required therapy. Vulnerability is a requirement for human connection, but it's not easy.

Essentially, most of society is on autopilot and enjoying the blissful naivete of the "blue pill" they subconsciously selected by running away from vulnerability. The real culprit is the fact that they subconsciously believe they are not lovable, just like Will Hunting. Shame and fear control them because of this fundamental belief. As a result, their paradigm gets stuck and creates other limiting beliefs instead of facing the 800-pound gorilla!

According to Brené Brown, "Vulnerability is the core of shame and fear and our struggle for worthiness but it is also the birth place of joy, creativity, belonging and love." She describes this realization as being "a yearlong street fight that I resisted and eventually lost but won my life back." This sounds quite similar to Will Hunting's struggle with being vulnerable. Self-awareness is not just a decision, but an arduous journey—and the reward is massive.

Brown believes the problem is that, despite our attempt to do so, humans cannot selectively numb specific feelings without numbing our other emotions. We inadvertently also numb joy, gratitude, and happiness. This subconsciously leads to us feeling miserable and searching for purpose and meaning—that same feeling Neo felt in *The Matrix*. This happens because we lack human connections.

Brown states that connection, the ability to feel connected, is neuro-biological. It's core to our being. It's how we are wired (Brown, 2021). This process creates a vicious and dangerous cycle, unless we're vulnerable and free ourselves from the stuck paradigms and limiting beliefs resulting from disconnection.

If you are not vulnerable via transparent discussions and fully exploring your own paradigm, then System One will take over and use shortcuts leading to cognitive biases, creating limiting beliefs about yourself and others. Your paradigm will be stuck on a personal view of incorrect reality and not in tune with actual reality.

A LIBERATING "FAILURE" TO A STUCK PARADIGM

I used to think graduating from HBS was the crowning achievement of my life—the pinnacle and final climb of a goal I set in middle school. I achieved "success" by transforming myself from an impoverished immigrant into a professional via great education.

I defined myself by my affiliation with HBS after being admitted. It felt impossible not to, as it's seen by most people as the pre-eminent university and management program in the world. Even though I had also attended the number one hotel management program globally, The Cornell Hotel School, HBS became part of my paradigm of success.

Shortly after graduation, I learned out of over 100 alumni clubs, real estate was not one of them. I could not believe the strongest global real estate network was not formally organized. I recall thinking, *Anyone can start a company, but only one person ever can start the HBS Real Estate Alumni Association.* I proudly decided to be that person.

I reached out to the Alumni Club's team and created the required business plan, demonstrating a financially sustainable strategy and interest from the alumni body. The ten alumni club leaders and the global board of directors I recruited were impressive. I felt like the founder of a top start-up venture.

From the beginning, the club was a resounding success. Events were well attended and profitable. I prioritized the organization over my career efforts; this was my legacy, and I spared no time or expense to ensure success. I was deeply committed to adding value to alums.

The HBS Alumni Club team was supportive. The director was friendly, empathetic, and an inspirational leader. She made us feel appreciated as she was approachable, helpful, and proactively communicated with us. Everything changed when she accepted another job.

Out of the blue, I received a request to meet with the new director. We met at a seating area in the lobby of the famed Waldorf Astoria Hotel in Midtown Manhattan. I expected the meeting was to express gratitude for my many years of volunteer work for the school. Instead, I was blown away when the new director asked me to step down.

It was obvious he did not believe the bogus excuse he gave: that I had served for four years, a limit for club presidents. I had a friend who had been president of another club for about two decades. I knew others still in the role for well over that term. What was more telling was how the new director spoke condescendingly, with an air of superiority that made it clear I was not on his list of favorites. I could feel the discomfort and disapproval of his comments and demeanor from his colleague sitting next to him. Something was amiss.

One extremely wealthy alumnus from a powerful family had organized numerous events prior to the club's founding and thought I was stepping on his toes. He had close connections inside the school and with powerful outside alumni donors, including someone that had a strong say in school matters. Another alumnus led a real estate club for another institution and wanted to do the same here because it was a much larger profile brand and alumni body.

A new president from my own board of directors was installed who was friendly with the director. Interestingly, he decided not to work with any of my leadership team (save for one person supportive of what was happening), as if to erase all of our efforts. He created a significantly larger and even more impressive board of directors than we had, including the who's who of the industry. Plans were communicated about upcoming exuberant growth.

However, it was a catastrophic failure. Whereas we had a great leadership team and executed dozens of events worldwide, achieving significant success over the past four-year period, the new team held three events and then the club completely died but for some strategy sessions about what to do next. To my regret, they caused my legacy to fail. My communication with HBS over the years attempting to prevent the club's eternal demise fell on deaf ears.

This "failure" created the beginning of my self-awareness journey. It was my first perceived failure. I did not want to talk about it with anyone or face it. It felt shameful and debilitating. I felt betrayed and disconnected from the school. My paradigm was stuck.

I went from feeling like I was on the pinnacle of success to the bottom of failure, and I blamed my decision to volunteer for HBS. I regretted prioritizing my efforts to create and establish a club on the school's behalf. I couldn't understand how years of effort and success resulted in getting jettisoned from an organization adding significant value for alumni.

My efforts to understand the situation led to eventually realizing it was a case of classism and, and possibly, racism, as described to me by other alums with more information, but it took a lot of work and effort to get to the truth. I spoke with several people at the school and never received an official answer. The bogus reason provided by the director was never uttered again. I can only assume he lied.

I freed myself from this debilitating sentiment via extensive discussions with a cross section of people, related and not related to the situation. It required extensive vulnerability and looking at myself in the mirror. I hired an executive coach and he recommended other self-awareness courses that I dove into. I took a keen interest in the subject and read books, watched TED talks, and studied my actions and reactions to interaction and triggers.

I reflected deeply on the HBS situation and was honest with myself about what happened. I faced my fear, and I eventually concluded that HBS did not betray me. It was not personal. The school had a bad leader who made poor decisions, perhaps to keep or secure more donations for the school. HBS is a great institution that adds much value to society, but I remain disappointed that leaders were not more open and transparent with me. At the end of the day, every institution, business, or organization is comprised of flawed people with their own paradigms and biases. HBS put the wrong leader in charge, but fortunately it did not take them long to replace him.

I redefined success and what purpose and meaning meant in my life. Eventually, the experience was a distasteful "red pill," a second dose that liberated me to see life and myself more holistically. My paradigms about HBS and myself were limited and clouded by my strong identification with the school as my definition of success.

What I needed was first to expand my mindset and understand failure at a greater level, from my own lens. I also needed to understand it was not personal. Once I had the courage to do that, I had to define it for myself in a way that worked for me. What I realized was that "failure" was a mental construct—a harsh self-judgment derived from the perception about the value or state of others' efforts; a negative judgment of other's actions, efforts or perspective.

Failure was a harsh self-limiting belief I got from a societal paradigm. I now believe what many have written on the subject: failure is a great launching pad to success. I freed my paradigm from the negative emotions created by my belief that a goal was not accomplished.

I now understand that my most significant accomplishment was choosing to become self-aware and to learn about myself and how humans and society work. HBS is an important part of my journey for sure, but it's one of many variables in the equation.

"We cannot change anything until we accept it. Condemnation does not liberate, it oppresses."

—CARL JUNG

YOUR PARADIGMS ARE YOUR RESPONSIBILITY

As I was forced to discover by HBS, your paradigm is your responsibility. You can choose the "blue pill" and ignore it at your peril. If you do, you will be subjecting yourself to the subconscious and irrational control of your past experiences and emotions, which create automatic, outdated mental shortcuts. If you don't, you can choose to acknowledge, understand, and cultivate your paradigm for greater access to power and a more fulfilling journey through life, offering the ability to add value to your relationships and society.

"Just because something's not your fault doesn't mean it's not your responsibility. Our ability to act and change is proportional to the amount of responsibility we take on for ourselves" (Mark Manson Tweet, August 24, 2021).

When my son was in the fourth grade, I signed him up for track. He was not thrilled with the sport and complained, telling his friends and coaches I "was forcing him" to do it. Since track helped me become a stronger, more resilient person, I wanted to bestow the benefits upon him. My goal for him was to be in track until the eighth grade; however, after two years of witnessing meager effort, I tried another strategy.

I gave him a choice: "Try your absolute best, and then you decide whether you run track or not. But if you do not do your best, you are doing it until eighth grade." He could not believe his ears, as he saw a way to curtail his track tenure. He wholeheartedly agreed. The entire following season, Nathaniel didn't run a race in which he was not first or second in his heat. His coaches marveled at the transformation. My wife and I gleamed with pride, not at his placement, but at the fact that he was trying his best. Our motto is we will always be proud if he just tries his absolute best in everything he does, regardless of the outcome.

I believe we all act this way. Once we make ourselves responsible for outcomes, our performance meaningfully improves. Our actions have a purpose, and we know where we are going. Life becomes more intentional and more organized.

But this is not enough. "Without developing a clear vision of the future we desire, of the values we want to adopt, of the identities we want to shed or step into—we are forever doomed to repeat the failures of our past" (Mark Manson Tweet August 25, 2021). We have to be specific about our goals so we can hold ourselves accountable, learn from our successes and failures, and change them when necessary. If we don't know where we are going, we will never get there and we will not enjoy the journey.

Do not be a static version of yourself. You must keep working on yourself to maximize your life's productivity, value, and happiness. The journey of self-awareness and cultivating your paradigm is a dynamic and empowering journey full of mistakes, failures, success, and joy. The negative aspects of the journey give meaning to the positive ones.

FROM STUCK PARADIGM TO GLOBAL CLIMATE CHANGE LEADER

Greta Thunberg, the international sensation who has created the most significant climate activism in history, has a very unique paradigm impacted by her Asperger's Syndrome, which she acknowledges as a disability but also considers her "superpower" (Rourke, 2019). When Greta was about eleven years old, one of her teachers showed the class a video about the detrimental impacts of climate change that resulted in her paradigm getting stuck.

As would be expected, not long after watching the video, her classmates moved on to other interests. Greta, however, could not move on and fell into a deep state of depression. She felt extremely lonely and could not comprehend how humans were unconcerned in light of this devastating and urgent threat to our planet.

"I couldn't understand how that could exist, that existential threat, and yet we didn't prioritize it," she said. "I was maybe in a bit of denial, like, 'That can't be happening, because if that were happening, then the politicians would be taking care of it'" (Alter, 2019).

This period, which she refers to as her "endless sadness," persisted despite her parents doing everything they could to make her feel better, including taking time off work. Greta battled depression for many months and stopped eating and talking while her parents consulted doctors, but nothing worked. Her father told her that all would be fine, but after researching the matter, realized he was wrong. "I realized that she was right, and I was wrong, and I had been wrong all my life," Svante told *TIME*.

As a way to bring their daughter back from depression, the family changed their habits and became more environmentally conscious, including eating less meat, growing their own vegetables, not flying, and installing solar panels, among other things. "We did all these things, basically, not really to save the climate, we didn't care much about that initially. We did it to make her happy and to get her back to life" (Alter, 2019).

Taking action worked and Greta began to feel better. In 2018, a climate change essay she wrote was published in a newspaper in Sweden. It was at around this same time that the students from Marjory Stoneman Douglas High School in Parkland, Florida were organizing to protest gun violence. When a Scandinavian climate activist contacted Greta after reading her article, she suggested they organize school strikes against climate change, just like those high school students.

The activists decided against the idea, so Greta made up her mind to strike alone (*Democracy Now!*, 2018). She informed her parents she would go on strike to put pressure on the government of Sweden to honor the goals of the Paris Agreement.

This was the start of Greta's successful "Skolstrejk för klima-tet" campaign, which translates to "School Strike for Climate."

"Learning about climate change triggered my depression in the first place," she recounts. "But it was also what got me out of my depression, because there were things I could do to improve the situation. I don't have time to be depressed anymore." According to her father, when she began striking, she "came back to life."

Can you imagine being eleven years old and learning that humans are destroying the planet and killing themselves, and no one really cares? If you felt your life was in imminent danger, how would you feel? Paradigms hold the algorithm for the creation of our emotions.

It is hard to believe, but your emotions and your reality are created by your paradigms.

Greta's reality became a state of depression and powerless-ness. Her normal paradigm was in a state of crisis or disbelief. Her view of society no longer held true. Humans could not be allowing this to happen, right? In her mind, everyone she loved, including herself, was set for self-destruction.

She needed a paradigm from which to function, so just like scientists calculated that the world was in fact round, not flat, she became the paradigm revolution for society by shifting her paradigm from one of fear to one of action, an act that was extremely liberating and empowering for her.

Just a few years since she started striking, Greta has become the leading climate activist in history and its loudest voice. What started out as a small, single voice with a homemade sign and no followers is now a "Great Thunder" for change, reminding the rest of us that climate change is the single greatest priority of our time.

In her 2018 TED Talk, Greta described her perspective: "I was diagnosed with Asperger's Syndrome, OCD, and selective mutism. That basically means I only speak when I think it's necessary." In Greta's paradigm, our existence depends on her voice, because we are not acting like we are endangering our planet. "You say you love your children above all else," Greta warned at the UN Climate Change Conference in Poland in 2018, "and yet you are stealing their future in front of their very eyes" (Sutter, 2018).

In 2019, a sixteen-year-old Greta told world leaders at the UN General Assembly in New York that "we are in the beginning of a mass extinction, and all you can talk about is money and fairy tales of eternal economic growth. How dare you" (Green, 2019)?

What began as local effort in front of the Swedish Parliament is now a major global movement. Children all over the world have joined the School Strike Movement. Millions of people have joined demonstrations and climate strikes around the world because of her. She is celebrated frequently and has made friends and supporters, such as Pope Francis, Al Gore, and numerous presidents and leaders around the world, including fellow youth activist, Malala Yousafzai. *TIME* named her Person of the Year in 2019, the same year she was nominated for the Nobel Peace Prize by three members of the committee. Margaret Atwood—the Canadian poet, novelist, literary critic, essayist, teacher, environmental activist, and inventor—compared her to Joan of Arc (Burgess, 2019).

Her celebrity has also won her much criticism by global leaders that are climate change deniers, such as Russian President Vladimir Putin, former US president Donald Trump, and Brazilian President Bolsonaro (Rowlatt, 2020/Britton, 2019). However, despite the hate aimed at her, she remains unfazed. "I think that [their criticism is] a good sign actually," she says, "because that shows we are actually making a difference and they see us as a threat" (Alter, 2019). Her comments are evidence of a powerful paradigm in sync with reality.

SO, WHAT ARE THE IMPLICATIONS TO YOUR PARADIGM?

The way I interpret Brené Brown's research in regard to paradigms is that the more numb we become from not being vulnerable and sharing our thoughts and experiences with others, the more disconnected we get from other humans and from reality. We limit the full context an expanded paradigm provides. We unconsciously limit our paradigms in an attempt to avoid shame and fear (and connect with each other), but instead we invite a series of other issues into our lives and the world.

This leads to the "you are wrong, and I am right" mentality that disconnects us in regard to politics, climate change, abortion, race, immigration, and other important yet controversial societal issues. We pretend what we do doesn't have an impact on other people, our environment, and our world.

We transform ourselves into powerless beings on autopilot, as if in a dream state, and put our heads in the sand.

Brené Brown is describing a society stuck on specific paradigms based on their unwillingness to authentically share their thoughts and experiences with each other (their paradigms). Can you imagine how scientifically backward we would be if scientists, instead of collaborating and working with each other via extensive authentic dialogue aimed at solving specific scientific issues, refused to share information out of fear or shame? We would probably still be cavemen. But Greta Thunberg is proving that, as individuals, we are doing this—even to the detriment of the planet.

Unfortunately, except for science, business, and other subjects requiring us to collaborate externally, that is not how we normally operate in regard to sharing our internal thoughts and opinions of ourselves; however, if we expand our human paradigms and authentically share our thoughts and experiences vulnerably in the manner of Brené's wholehearted groups, imagine how advanced and utopian our society could be today. We would be able to rapidly eradicate poverty, hunger, climate risks, and other perils to our species and planet.

We would all collectively expand our paradigms and move society forward in amazing ways we cannot even fathom.

Principle 3: Practice genuine vulnerability with key close friends to eliminate limiting beliefs.

CHAPTER 4

Vulnerability as the Antidote to Stuck Paradigms

"Nothing in life is to be feared. It is only to be understood."

—MARIE CURIE

The Breakfast Club is an American cult classic movie addressing major societal issues facing our country—specifically, it addresses the impact of loneliness on our mental health, happiness, and meaning/purpose.

Several students from different walks of life, gender, social groups, and diverse perspectives come together for detention on a Saturday morning. The only characteristic they have in common is a sense of disconnection—from each other, from their parents, and from most of society—which detrimentally impacts their lives.

At the start of detention, they fight, argue, curse, and generally mistreat each other. They are disturbed members of society for the most part and cannot get along.

The school's principal treats them with disdain and views them as what is wrong with society. They soon find a common foe in the principal and unite against him, sharing several experiences that begin to bond them together.

With nine hours of detention, they are forced to spend much time together in the same space. Out or boredom, they start to share and probe deep into each other's lives, passive aggressively at first, but eventually with more respect. While most resist vulnerability, eventually they give in and come to truly know each other and create true bonds.

Some of the information divulged is shocking but leads to establishing even closer connections. What they all have in common is that none feel truly loved or accepted by their parents. As a result, they do not feel worthy of love. Sharing their paradigms with each other so vulnerably creates a strong bond between them. It allows them to expand their perspectives and appreciate each other, themselves, and their life journey more.

While they walk into the school as moody strangers at seven a.m., they leave the grounds with power, happily and as close friends whose paradigms have shifted. They were exactly the same people, but the act of being truly vulnerable changed their perspectives on life for their benefit, as well as their friends', families', and society's.

THE INCREASING LONELINESS AND
DISCONNECTION PANDEMIC

In 2017, former US Surgeon General Vivek Murthy called loneliness a public health "epidemic" (Sweet, 2021). Loneliness has for decades been a global issue, but COVID-19 and technological advances have exacerbated the situation. We are fortunate President Joseph Biden again called him to service as the twenty-first US surgeon general in 2021. Murthy has had a long career as a public health physician and advocate.

Prior to becoming Surgeon General, Dr. Murthy co-founded several organizations. VISIONS is a global HIV/AIDS education organization. The Swasthya Project is a rural health partnership that trained women in South India to become community health workers and educators. TrialNetworks is a technology company dedicated to improving collaboration and efficiency in clinical trials. Dr. Murthy also founded Doctors for America, a nonprofit mobilizing physicians and medical students to improve access to affordable care.

His scientific research has focused on vaccine development and the participation of women and minorities in clinical trials. He was an internal medicine doctor at Brigham and Women's Hospital in Boston and at Harvard Medical School, where he attended thousands of patients and trained undergraduates, medical students, and medical residents over numerous years (HHS.gov, 2021).

A renowned physician, research scientist, entrepreneur, and author of the bestselling book, *Together: The Healing Power of Human Connection in a Sometimes Lonely World*, Dr. Murthy is among the most trusted voices discussing issues regarding public health. That is why when he speaks about a pandemic of loneliness and disconnection, we must listen and heed his warnings.

Dr. Murthy's experience as a surgeon general under the Obama Administration required him to travel across the country speaking to a diverse group people. He arrived at a worrisome realization: the loneliness epidemic is a major problem in society, one correlated with drug abuse, crime, mental health, and a series of other problems. As described in his book, according to an AARP study, 22 percent of US adults report being socially isolated. Figures are similar throughout the globe. He believes loneliness is about more than just being physically alone. He defines loneliness as the sense that you lack the connections you need (Murthy, 2020).

Dr. Murthy describes loneliness as an evolutionary mechanism telling us something is wrong, an idea also discussed by Professor John Cacioppo, who has studied the effects and causes of loneliness for over twenty-five years. Basically, our early ancestors sensed real physical danger from loneliness. Isolation placed them at risk of being killed by predators. Our bodies have not evolved past this feeling and loneliness creates an unconscious trigger, stressing the body and mind, as if we're really in danger of death. It's another outdated mental process that ignites unconscious automatic responses from our bodies.

Murthy describes loneliness as being paradoxical. If we are hungry or thirsty, we will eat or drink; if we are lonely, instead of seeking connection, we shy away from it. As stated before, Murthy believes this is an evolutionary response to a potential threat for ancient man, who would have stayed away from danger. However, avoiding danger in today's environment is equivalent to walking right into it by choosing not to connect.

Cacioppo, the director of the University of Chicago's Center for Cognitive and Social Neuroscience, agrees. In his book *Loneliness: Human Nature and the Need for Social Connection*, he examines the pathology and public health implications of the subject. In a 2016 interview for *The Guardian* moderated by Tim Adams, Cacioppo warned that "loneliness is like an iceberg—it goes deeper than we can see."

He also states that "the brain is the organ for creating, monitoring, nurturing, and retaining these social connections, so it didn't matter whether you actually had these connections, what was important was whether you felt that you had them. There is a big difference between objective isolation and perceived isolation, and very quickly we learned that perceived isolation was loneliness, and that had not been studied." What this means is that loneliness comes from your personal reality, and just the belief that one is lonely causes repercussions. Unfortunately, the consequences of loneliness are massive and are both mental and physical.

Cacioppo believes "loneliness is contagious, heritable, affects one in four people—and increases the chances of early death by 20 percent."

He also believes loneliness is a universal trait. "Loneliness is heritable, we have discovered. The sociality that is designed into our brains and DNA therefore has individual variation. In terms of the heritability of loneliness, we have taken that to mean disconnection is differentially painful. Some people it hardly bothers at all, some people it disturbs so much as to become a pathology. Those that aren't bothered at all may well be psychopaths."

In an article for *Vox* written by Roge Karma, Murthy said, "What we see with loneliness—and also with addiction—is that when we feel shame around some aspect of our life, it drives us further inward and chips away at our self-esteem. When you're lonely, what you need most of all is to reach out and connect with others. But the shame around loneliness pushes you in exactly the opposite direction. The longer your loneliness persists, the harder it is to reach out to other people because you don't feel you're worthy. This is why the downward spiral of loneliness is very challenging to break."

Like Dr. Murthy, Cacioppo believes loneliness is a pandemic affecting all of society. Our modern world is exacerbating the problem via technological advances. These tech improvements eliminate or reduce the need to physically interact—food delivery apps keep us at home, for example.

Dr. Murthy believes the solution to this pandemic is developing the right mix of relationships and he describes the long-term *Harvard University Study of Adult Development* that I discuss in chapter eleven.

However, the only way to truly solve these issues is to invoke System Two thinking and bring rational awareness at a societal level. Doing so will transport our evolutionary response to modern times, or at least provide us with the paradig-matic awareness to understand and process the sensorial outputs of loneliness to mitigate the negative physical and mental detriments.

UNDERSTAND FEAR, THEN CONQUER IT

Unfortunately, the pandemic of loneliness and its repercus-sions cannot be solved en mass. We have to choose to be both aware of the root issues as well as decide to address them individually, as they are part of our paradigms.

Based on Brené Brown's work and our paradigm framework so far, we now know that disconnection is an unintended consequence of a desire for connection—a mistake caused by fear. I believe the source of that fear is a subconscious, fundamental belief that we're not worthy of love.

It's that sense of "I'm not good enough" or "something is wrong with this world" that so many of us experience. We will speak more about this later in the chapter, but what this means is, for the majority of people, the desire for human connection is so strong that the fear of rejection if they are transparent also leads them to fear vulnerability.

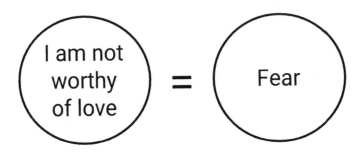

This is problematic, because what Brené Brown found is that it's actually the act of being vulnerable and revealing our true selves to others that results in authentic human connection. While the practicality of the plot of *The Breakfast Club* is questionable, the movie accurately demonstrates the human connections created by vulnerability. A group of strangers and misfits share themselves transparently and become close friends, more accepting and appreciative of each other.

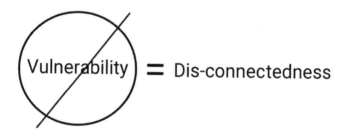 = Dis-connectedness

I am going to expand on Brené Brown's excellent work by postulating that limiting beliefs arise out of disconnection as the individual's way of manifesting the reality they see through their own specific paradigm. They believe they are unlovable, and as a result, they fear being their true selves because they don't believe they are worthy of love (but want to be loved). Thus, they reject vulnerability, choosing to present what they think is a more lovable version of themselves. As a result, they are then unable to truly connect with other humans.

Not being authentic makes them unlovable since vulnerability is the doorway to love. We must let people into our authentic paradigms to truly connect. We can do so inauthentically, and it may work temporarily, but once the lie is discovered, the connection is severed, likely for the long term. Distrust kills vulnerability.

Furthermore, we ourselves would know we are being inauthentic, preventing us from feeling connected. As a result, the failure to be vulnerable leads to disconnectedness from other people and from ourselves, and this in turn is what creates limiting beliefs about ourselves. As Dr. Murthy and Cacioppo insinuate and as Brené Brown stated, this feeling of disconnection leads to serious societal problems, including but not limited to drug abuse, obesity, and a lack of purpose and meaning that have grave implications for humanity.

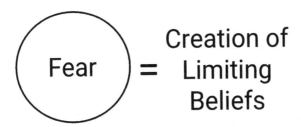

In essence, inauthenticity reinforces our false belief that we're not good enough, though we don't understand how we create that reality inadvertently. It's an awful "blue pill" to swallow, but in our personal paradigm, the evidence is overwhelming. It would be natural to say to yourself, "I felt I was unworthy of love and other people don't have an interest in connecting with me, so I must be right." Since we cannot be honest with ourselves or others when we operate from a paradigm of limiting beliefs (lies about ourselves, others, and reality), we become inauthentic.

Also possible for people with stuck paradigms who are inauthentic, say openly racist people, is vulnerable connection over their limiting beliefs. Some of the far-right groups, like militias, result from people discovering they can connect and be valued in these fringe organizations. One danger in how we confront loneliness is in manufacturing a less lonely reality instead of planning how to have a healthy one.

When we look at some of the people prosecuted for the January 6, 2021 riot, we see they were willing to do things they later saw as wrong just to stay connected to the social reality they had created. Eventually these twisted and inauthentic reasons to connect become destructive, as they are not acceptable to a functioning society or to people in sync with true reality.

$$\left(\text{Fear}\right) = \begin{array}{c}\text{Creation of}\\\text{Limiting}\\\text{Beliefs}\end{array} = \begin{array}{c}\text{Inauthentic}\\\text{Self}\end{array}$$

Our subconscious conclusion is that if we're not good enough for others, we're not good enough for ourselves either. The cycle is vicious and repeats itself over and over and over again. Essentially, the paradigm is stuck on "I am not worthy of love" and we become slaves to a numb and meaningless life! The feeling of being unworthy of love and the resulting fear and shame is a vicious virus that invades and infects most, if not all, of our other paradigms.

We become cynical and operate from a state of numbness, creating a negative life perspective and operating on auto-pilot. We activate sleep mode because the truth we see is too painful and life loses its meaning. That's when we start looking for meaning and purpose in life. I also believe a stuck paradigm that is definitional to your life, even if you don't have the "I'm not worthy" feeling, can lead to this path as well. It describes my feelings after I felt betrayed by HBS.

The highly infectious, vicious cycle of the "I am not worthy of love" stuck paradigm looks like this:

From this sense of "I am not worthy of love," fear emerges, making us afraid to be our vulnerable true selves, preventing human connections, and creating limiting beliefs. As we discussed in the last chapter, you have to explore your paradigms and look for the negative feelings that indicate where a paradigm is stuck. The subconscious or conscious belief that "I'm not worthy of love" is a major obstacle for the creation of adequate human connections.

While you may not realize it, this has a detrimental impact on your life, those you love, and society (as you will add less or negative value). You must become aware of and speak with others about this feeling. To understand it, you must find the source of this feeling so you can expand your paradigm and free yourself from this enslaving, numbing reality that severely clouds your lenses.

As a general rule, fear will always lead you down the wrong path and result in stuck paradigms unless faced!

Fear must be confronted, fought, and defeated. I will show you how later in the chapter, but you may also want to consider whether professional therapy would be appropriate.

> *"He who is not every day conquering some*
> *fear has not learned the secret of life."*
>
> —RALPH WALDO EMERSON

MY CONNECTION TO THE REAL WORLD

For over ten years I have been part of a Harvard Business School Alumni forum, a group of fellow HBS alums that get together monthly to share our paradigms as they relate to personal life, family, and careers. Our background of relatedness is that we attended the same business school, but we didn't know each other before forming this group.

Confidentiality is of the utmost importance—what is shared in the group stays in the group. We are a diverse group in the pure sense of the word. About half are female, some are international, and our social-economic backgrounds are varied. Professionally, some work in business and some work for nonprofit organizations, while others decided to stay home to care for their children. The youngest is about twelve years apart for age from the oldest. Some have no children and some have college-aged kids.

We have witnessed each other change jobs, have children, find and marry spouses, lose jobs, start businesses, succeed, fail, cry, laugh, and all other normal life changes that occur. We are close, but not the type of friends that attend each other's birthday parties, weddings, or other personal occasions.

My HBS forum was invaluable in helping me deal with the HBS betrayal experiences and other key issues hiding in my paradigm. As an example, I became aware of several unconscious biases I did not know I had by sharing my thoughts and having my colleagues respond from their own perspective.

The goal of the group is sharing experiences without judgment—ensuring we are not giving direct advice—in a manner allowing us to expand each other's perspectives so we can better understand and appreciate our own. We have all been deeply vulnerable with each other and have committed to this group for the long term. No discussion or topic is rejected and we each present on life matters we need help with occasionally.

Without a doubt, this has been the most paradigm-expanding experience of my life! I believe this way of sharing experiences with a diverse group has made me a better person, made me a better father, improved my career, and allowed me to overcome obstacles in my life. I can honestly say the ability to vulnerably share myself with others has allowed me to connect deeper with loved ones and myself and to understand my paradigms better. I am a better person because of this group.

> *"I'm not afraid of storms, for I'm*
> *learning how to sail my ship."*
>
> —LOUISA MAY ALCOTT

A LIGHT SHINING OUT OF THE TUNNEL

This is an amazing revelation in case you have not caught it yet. To free yourself from the chains of all stuck paradigms, to be alive, powerful, and in control of your emotions and your life, all you have to do is have the courage to be vulnerable and reveal your true self to others!

If you want to free your paradigms, unleash an incredible amount of power for yourself, and create powerful human connections, the fundamental concept that unifies all human behavior and emotions is active, repetitive, and authentic vulnerability, which will expose your limiting beliefs and free and expand your paradigms! This is what that would look like in graph form:

But wait, there is one fundamental piece of the formula still missing for many of us. Why do people feel unworthy of love to begin with? Is this a conscious or unconscious belief? Whose love are we unworthy of and does that matter? Why are so many people infirm with this affliction? From my experience and observation, my answer is that when you were young, for legitimate or misinterpreted reasons, you didn't "feel" that your parents genuinely loved you, as was the case with the members of *The Breakfast Club*. You became convinced they did not really love you and that made you unworthy of *all* love. If your own parents don't love you, then who can really love you, since family is everything?

Other people may have had a distinct experience. They may have never questioned their parents' love, and their shame and fear of rejection came from experiences with someone else, such as a romantic partner, a sibling, a close friend, another authority figure (teacher, mentor, other family member), or their perception of God. A difficult experience with people to whom we are emotionally attached or choosing to do something we believe disconnects us from God can also lead to a feeling of being unworthy of love.

The issue with this thought process is that we can barely understand our own paradigms. Thus, our unexplored *assumptions* of the feelings of others from our insufficient paradigmatic lenses are only that: assumptions. Assumptions are not a basis for nor based on reality. This reason is exactly why Kuhn invented his five-step cycle process. Based on his assumptions, Aristotle's work was simple and elementary. Kuhn later understood when he looked at the issue from Aristotle's paradigm, which required extensive research and discussion to make sure he had it right, Aristotle's scientific paradigm was in fact advanced for his time—that's why he was considered such a genius and the father of science (Kuhn, 1987).

Similarly, we have to try to understand our parents' paradigm as widely as possible and it requires a scientific process based on fact, not mere assumptions. This would include extensive dialogue and observation of their actions.

FROM JUDGMENT TO CONNECTION

Understanding my father's paradigm was essential for me to connect with him, develop an authentic relationship, and understand his life from his eyes. There was a time I questioned whether my father loved me.

Based on my perception and observations, his actions didn't demonstrate love and affection for me. A man of few words and limited expressions of love or any other sentiments, my dad is best described as a traditional Dominican husband and father, for those of you with the paradigm to understand what that means (culture can be quite paradigmatic, as is language). What he said, what he did not say, and his actions pointed to a lack of love.

When I was in high school, my father became an entrepreneur after the restaurant where he was a chef closed. It was summertime and I was working with him. He and some partners acquired a restaurant in Queens, NY, and we had to drive some twenty-five minutes from our apartment in lower Manhattan to get to work. Throughout that entire summer, after nearly one-hundred car rides to and from work, I don't believe my dad said more than a dozen words to me. There was minimal attempt at conversation. I viewed this as a lack of interest in having a relationship with me.

My father has never in his life said "I love you" to me. He has a quick temper. When we were young and mischievous, all he had to do was look at us and we would stop making noise or misbehaving. I have no recollection of being hugged or of him displaying loving affection toward me. He believes his children have to respect what he says and not speak back to him. My father never attended any of my sporting events and practically had to be begged to attend my high school, college, and business school graduations.

It would have been easy for me to conclude that he did not love me and disconnect from our relationship. I probably would have, if not for the fact that my mother provides sufficient loving for two parents. She is the glue keeping us all united and together. She creates balance from a parental perspective and made up for a lot of my dad's shortcomings.

I was still in high school when I made the effort to understand my father and really listen to his story. I had no understanding of paradigms at the time, but I was being purposeful in trying to see life from his point of view so my judgment of his actions would be fair.

I asked him deep, probing questions and really listened to what he had to say in a way that I couldn't have done without love hanging in the balance. The result was that my feelings for him were strengthened. The judgment I created from my personal lenses was wrong.

I learned he was giving us much more love than he had ever received. My father was one of twenty-nine children. As was usual at the time for the lower classes in the country, my grandfather did not marry. He lived with some partners throughout their relationships. When my father was born, or shortly thereafter, my grandfather was no longer in a relationship with my dad's mother.

When dad was two years old, his mother went to a party and his dad was so upset "she was not properly taking care of him" that he took him away from her to live with him and his partner.

My father didn't know who his real mother was until he was eighteen years old.

His adopted mother, whom he believed was his real mother, treated him harsher and showed favoritism to his younger brother, her real son. Though his dad was protective of my father, he would travel for work and was not around often. There was ample opportunity for my father's paradigm to be detrimentally impacted.

My father got all the undesirable chores and became responsible for the majority of the farming starting at eight years old. His dad did a lot of traveling to sell farm goods in other parts of the country. He also spent his money and time on female conquests and "having fun." My father paid the repercussions of the actions of his parents at a very young age.

My father didn't feel loved by his adopted mother and that must have been traumatic. It was an unfair deal for them both. Imagine living with someone you believe is your mother and she secretly dislikes you because you're the son of another woman—and imagine having to raise the child of your partner's ex.

My father tells a story about when he had a disease and was blind for several months at the age of twelve. Those must have been eternal months without a loving mother around.

Understanding my father's true paradigm allowed me to see why he is the way that he is. I'm extremely grateful he's the type of father that stuck around and did the best he could with the paradigm he has. Knowing how difficult he had it, I don't know how he could have done a better job.

I feel privileged he found the strength to love us as deeply as he does (even if he doesn't show it). I did not start the quest from this perspective, but my expanded paradigm allows me to see reality versus my judgments of someone else from my own paradigm. I feel like my relationship with my dad meaningfully improved since we had that discussion. I routinely ask him questions about his past to connect with him. Vulnerability has deepened our relationship.

SO WHAT DOES THIS MEAN FOR YOUR PARADIGM?

Vulnerability is the doorway to processing limiting negative beliefs impacting how we feel about ourselves and life. These unprocessed negative feelings destroy us from the inside. The detrimental repercussions are mental and physical. They don't go away until addressed but limit potential while they exist. It is essential for us to be honest with ourselves and both face and reveal these feelings to people we love and trust. Refusing to do so will have severely negative consequences not only on you, but also on your relationships and your ability to manifest your definition of success and add value in life.

Now that you have awareness of your personal paradigms and how you can unleash a tremendous amount of power from expanding or shifting them, over the next few chapters we will dive deeper into limiting beliefs, self-awareness, authenticity, and finding your true self.

Principle 4: Face your fears to avoid the creation of limiting beliefs and an inauthentic self.

CHAPTER 5

Shift Your Paradigm for Greater Access to Power

"It is in this space of mastery over paradigms that people throw off addictions, live in constant joy, bring down empires, get locked up or burn at the stake, or crucified or shot and have impacts that last for millennia."

—DONELLA MEADOWS (THINKING IN SYSTEMS: A PRIMER, 2008)

The beginning lyrics of the song "Alexander Hamilton" in the Broadway musical *Hamilton*, written by Lin-Manuel Miranda, are controversial. The song partially refers to Hamilton in derogatory terms, including "bastard" and "son of a whore." The point of the song, however, is to describe how, although he was born a poor immigrant from the Caribbean, through hard work and determination, he became a scholar and an American hero—a founding father of our great nation. This was an astounding feat for some-one from an impoverished and disreputable background at the time.

The play was a paradigm shift for the theater industry because it was written and performed by a cast of characters not nor-mally associated with US founding fathers, including immi-grants, African Americans, Asians, Latinos, and women. The music selection is also distinct in that it heavily utilizes hip hop, R&B, soul, and pop—in some sense, the music of the poor and the oppressed—to narrate the story of the creation of the United States of America. Miranda, who is Puerto Rican, described *Hamilton* as about "America then, as told by America now" (Delman, 2015).

From its opening, *Hamilton* received impressive critical acclaim (*The Economist*, 2015). It was definitely a new par-adigm for theater-goers and they absolutely loved the shift. The fact that the play was sold out for years, coupled with a hefty admissions price tag exceeding one thousand dollars, ironically made it inaccessible to the majority of the very people it represented, especially the poor and less well off.

When theaters closed due to the COVID-19 pandemic in 2020, a filmed version of the Broadway production was released on Disney+, making it accessible to the general population at a low cost relative to the live performance ticket price, as if by karma.

The truth is that Alexander Hamilton, one of the fathers of the United States of America, was in fact an impover-ished immigrant and an unlikely father of democracy. He overcame significant hurdles to become the person we know of today, as described in the Broadway musical.

This fascinating masterpiece tells the story of a true American hero, but one with a less-than-stellar reputation, if you go by society's paradigm at the time. In reality, first and foremost, Alexander Hamilton was an unstoppable survivor who cared for his fellow man and this nascent democracy, and who had lofty aspirations for himself as well as this great nation.

Interestingly though, from a political and power perspective, the founding of this promising nation was itself a paradigm shift. The dissatisfaction and need to break away from English rule created opportunities for nontraditional leaders to step into powerful roles typically reserved for wealthy elites.

This topic was explored by Joseph J. Ellis in his article "Founding Fathers—The Explanations," wherein he posed and answered the following question: "How did this backwoods province on the western rim of the Atlantic world, far removed from the epicentres of learning and culture in London and Paris, somehow produce thinkers and ideas that transformed the landscape of modern politics?"

I would dare say the impact was much greater than Ellis described. It revolutionized the world and shifted the balance of power to a young nation, creating a new global paradigm persisting today. It redefined political leadership.

Ellis refers to the early days of the US as "postaristocratic," because in England and Europe hereditary bloodlines, being part of the aristocracy was a requirement for serving in public office or in other positions of power and influence. There were few, if any, aristocrats in American society at the time, so it was a meritocracy by necessity, making talent more valuable than in Europe. This created a unique opportunity for Hamilton and others, such as Ben Franklin, who were considered political elites on the basis of their merit despite their impoverished backgrounds—a paradigm shift at the time created by the nascent stage of the new country.

As described by Ellis, "the Founders were a self-conscious elite unburdened by egalitarian assumptions. Their constituency was not 'the people' but 'the public,' which they regarded as the long-term interest of the citizenry that they— the Founders—had been chosen to divine. Living between the assumptions of an aristocratic and a democratic world without belonging fully to either, the Founders maximized the advantages of both."

One of the most celebrated biographies of Hamilton was written by Ron Chernow, and this is the book that inspired Lin-Manuel Miranda to write the play *Hamilton*. Chernow "recounts Hamilton's turbulent life: an illegitimate, largely self-taught orphan from the Caribbean, he came out of nowhere to take America by storm, rising to become George Washington's aide-de-camp in the Continental Army, coauthoring The Federalist Papers, founding the Bank of New York, leading the Federalist Party, and becoming the first Treasury Secretary of the United States." He possessed a strong combination of ambition and tenacity that allowed him to add value to society in many ways.

Based on Alexander Hamilton's pivotal role and the numerous important responsibilities he held during the early years of this country, can you imagine what America and the world would look like today had he not had an expanded paradigm? It is inconceivable that we would be as great a nation without his extensive contributions. This American experiment may have already failed otherwise.

Now imagine the impact you can have on society, your family, or your definition of success if you choose to expand your paradigm in the meritocratic manner that Alexander Hamilton did. If only we could make our life journey as meaningful to one element of society as his was to the United States, what could we accomplish? What would your contributions look like?

MAKE LEMONADE WHEN SERVED LEMONS

As high school juniors, we had to meet with our college admissions counselor to discuss the upcoming application process. I was a top student, but not at the very top. In addition to academics and sports, I worked well over twenty hours a week for life's essentials. Academics were my priority, but I didn't know how to play the college acceptance game. I would be the first in my family to apply.

When I told my counselor I planned to apply to Cornell University, the six-foot-plus, stern Jesuit priest from an Irish background stared at me pensively for a few seconds. He then told me "the only way that you can get into Cornell is if they need more Hispanics up there." In retrospect, I recognize this was a racist statement, but I didn't take it as such at the time.

I took it as a personal challenge that likely woke up my System Two processes. I was upset anyone would try to limit my options. I had spent my life expanding them and would not be told by anyone what my potential was. It was not personal to me. I was not angry at him and did not feel betrayed by him, contrary to the HBS Alumni Clubs situation. He didn't know me and I was not the type to be stopped by other people's negative perspectives and opinions.

The Jesuits were mainly responsible for my growth paradigm, so I was perplexed by his biased comments. I became even more academically focused after this interaction and made it a point to understand the college admissions game. I diversified my sports resume by joining the wrestling team my senior year and obtained a part-time job at an educational nonprofit company since my only experience was in the restaurant industry. My grades improved even more.

Not only did I get into Cornell, but I was also accepted by every other college to which I applied.

My high school counselor lit a fire under me as far as my paradigm was concerned. He was likely partially responsible for my academic performance at Cornell, which eventually led to my HBS acceptance. I take motivation from anywhere I can get it.

Instead of allowing them to stop you, use negative input as a stimulus to achieve your goals.

OPTIMISM IS THE KEY TO RESILIENCE

According to Martin E.P. Seligman, the Zellerbach Family Professor of Psychology and director of the Positive Psychology Center at the University of Pennsylvania, the key to resilience is optimism. Seligman is also known as "the father of optimism" based on his decades of research on the subject. In his April 2011 *Harvard Business Review* magazine article, "Building Resilience," he states that over fifteen years of study by him and his colleagues led to the discovery that one third of people bounce back stronger from setbacks and personal adversity (including trauma), one third bounce back to normal levels, and the other third are detrimentally impacted by their experience, with their paradigms likely getting stuck.

"We discovered that people who don't give up have a habit of interpreting setbacks as temporary, local, and changeable ('It's going away quickly; it's just this one situation, and I can do something about it')," he wrote in the article, which is based on his book *Flourish: A Visionary New Understanding of Happiness and Well-Being* (Seligman, 2011).

This deep discovery led to further research and the creation of numerous programs, including the Penn Resilience Program (PRP) for students and Comprehensive Soldier Fitness (CSF), which, in partnership with the US Army, was tested on 1.1 million soldiers. CSF was created because Seligman told US General Casey that "the army could shift its distribution toward the growth end [the one third of people that bounce back stronger] by teaching psychological skills to stop the downward spiral that often follows failure." General Casey saw the great potential of this methodology and agreed to test the army, ordering the organization to measure resilience and also teach positive psychology to soldiers. His goal was to create a force as psychologically fit as it was physically fit (Seligman, 2011).

Interestingly, Marty Seligman's work actually began with studies of learned helplessness, a psychological condition he discovered in which a person (or an organism) suffers from a sense of powerlessness, arising from traumatic events or persistent failures (*Encyclopedia Britannica*, 2021). He first saw how dogs are damaged by feeling they have no way out of painful or uncomfortable situations and give up, even when opportunities to escape later arise. After this and other discoveries focusing on negative psychological aspects, Seligman then decided to focus on the positive side, where he has added significant value.

The benefits of positive psychology on our paradigms are massive. Imagine interacting with the world without the numerous biases, emotions, and limiting beliefs normally holding us back. It would be a paradigm shift in our thinking and our ability to take positive actions. The best example I have heard of to explain the benefits of positive psychology was in an awful research study conducted by a Harvard educated Johns Hopkins professor.

In the 1950s, Rick Culter did a horrible experiment on rats to help in understanding positive psychology and its impact on paradigms. A dozen rats were placed inside a half-empty water jar. They were allowed to swim until they gave up and drowned. On average, the rats survived for fifteen minutes.

In a follow-up experiment, the rats were rescued immediately after giving up. When they were placed in the jar a second time just a few minutes later, *they swam for sixty hours before giving up.*

That is an incredible *240 times longer* than the first time and is strong evidence of the power of persistence and resilience.

Fortunately, our lives are likely to never be as hopeless as those of the rats in the jar. We have strong support networks consisting of family, friends, mentors and, if need be, government agencies to help us in those critical times of need in our journey through life. If you are like me, it is difficult for you to ask others for help, but the truth is that loved ones are always there for you, even if you do not realize it. We are all rats in the follow-up experiments that will be pulled out and saved. This means we can be significantly more resilient than we can possibly imagine, just like those hopeful rats.

But the most important take away from the story is all that was needed for unbelievable resilience was hope—nothing else. If you can cultivate a positive paradigm, you can be unstoppable in your endeavors and surprise yourself regarding how much you can accomplish.

FIXED VS. GROWTH MINDSET

In her fascinating book, *Mindset: The New Psychology of Success*, Carol S. Dweck, PhD, the Lewis and Virginia Eaton Professor of Psychology at Stanford University, divides the world into two groups of people: those with a growth mindset and those with a fixed mindset. Prof. Dweck defined these two mindsets during an interview in 2012 as follows:

"In a fixed mindset students believe their basic abilities, their intelligence, their talents, are just fixed traits. They have a certain amount and that's that, and then their goal becomes to look smart all the time and never look dumb. In a growth mindset students understand that their talents and abilities can be developed through effort, good teaching, and persistence. They don't necessarily think everyone's the same or anyone can be Einstein, but they believe everyone can get smarter if they work at it" (Murehad, 2012).

Carol Dweck's work is genius and provides deep insights into our actions, successes, and achievements. Looking at it from my own view, I believe fixed and growth mindsets are actually each a distinct paradigm. Furthermore, I believe they can coexist depending on the topic at hand and the individual's experience, or lack thereof, with that specific topic. This means we have numerous paradigms, some of which are fixed and others in a state of growth. Our minds are essentially a sea of paradigms defining how we see and interact with the world, but each can be at a different life cycle.

For example, a student can have a paradigm of "I'm not good in math" that is fixed, but at the same time work at becoming a great soccer player via continuous efforts to improve his/her abilities on the field, thereby having a growth mindset in the sport. This mindset is determined by a combination of experiences, interactions, and beliefs. Based on my own personal experience, I also believe a fixed mindset can shift to a growth mindset and achieve a greater amount of power—a person experiences a paradigm shift on a specific topic. I see a fixed mindset as someone having gotten stuck based on their upbringing, a traumatic or hurtful experience, or just a choice to keep their head in the sand about a particular topic. Our polarized political situation is a strong example.

I have always believed intelligence was a product of effort, and generally speaking, everyone has the same mental ability, regardless of genetics, race, gender, or any other variable. This is a paradigm I have developed over many years through self-reflection, research, observations, discussions, debates with others, and experimentation. I have expanded my abilities in areas that I was not initially good at or had a limiting belief. As an example, in my youth I was introverted—very shy and not very social. For this reason, I developed a belief that I didn't want to be social or to network to succeed in life. I used my exceptional academic abilities to find success. When I applied to Harvard Business School and understood their admissions model, I finally realized the importance of networking for business success. Whereas other programs focused primarily on undergraduate GPA and GMAT scores for admissions, HBS also focused on emotional intelligence and social abilities. This fit right in with their model of "educating leaders that make a difference in the world" (HBS. edu, 2021).

This reality didn't just dawn on me. I found the MBA application process to be deeply introspective and a journey of self-discovery in itself. I was forced to admit to myself I didn't really believe I could succeed without networking but had a fear of it based on my experiences while growing up. Once my paradigm expanded to include this truth, I decided to overcome this hurdle and join networking organizations as well as work on my social skills. At HBS, I joined numerous clubs and was the co-president of the Hospitality and Travel Industry Club. I founded and led the HBS Real Estate Alumni Association, where I had to speak publicly all the time. What was once a limiting condition became a strength, but it required me to look at myself with honesty and to work hard to overcome a limited mental paradigm.

Let's take a closer look at intelligence, fixed and growth mindsets, and my view of Carol Dweck's work from my paradigm perspectives, which I believe expands on her research or at least looks at it from a different angle that put paradigms at the very center.

FIXED MINDSET ON INTELLIGENCE

According to Dweck, people with a "fixed mindset," as it relates to intelligence, think it's fixed or static and unable to change. To them, you are either born with intelligence or you're not—it's that simple. The problem with a fixed mindset is that people who see life from this limited or unexplored perspective pass this trait on to their children and perpetuate this limiting belief to future generations. They say things like "you're smart" or "you're intelligent" when children get good grades, and insinuate the opposite if they don't by saying things like "you're too smart to get Cs."

As a result, the child's perspective becomes all about appearing "smart" and avoiding looking dumb at all costs. Because parents have such an impact on our paradigms, as we will see below, this mindset becomes self-defining. It gets stuck and we limit our beliefs. The effort isn't the goal but appearing intelligent becomes the priority, so there is no focus on the process and journey of learning. Instead, they are looking for external acknowledgment that they are smart. Attention is the reward—especially compliments or acknowledgment of intelligence. Does this sound like someone you know? If so, are you able to tell that this person associates their identity with being recognized as intelligent? Does that person always want to be right or appear intelligent? How does that impact how you feel about them and their social relationships?

Because it would be useless if everyone was just as intelligent from that person's perspective, it becomes a competitive game of "I'm the most intelligent," which creates a mentality of "I am more intelligent that you, so you are dumb." It creates an "us versus them" limiting perspective. People with a fixed mindset on intelligence are offended by anything or anyone that would suggest they lack intelligence since it would indicate that they are dumb—a state they don't believe can be altered. They feel threatened by the accomplishments of others because our society highly values intelligence, so anyone who succeeds more is believed not to have earned it because they are not as intelligent. You can imagine how the paradigm of a person with a fixed mindset will clash often with basically everybody else's, with that person continuously grasping for self-worth and externally fighting everyone to prove they are more intelligent.

The issue is even more detrimental when someone believes they're *not* intelligent. Their efforts mirror their limiting self-belief, and they give up most of their power in life. They will not aspire to succeed or accomplish much since they "lack" the intelligence to do it. These types of paradigm limitations normally develop when parents tell their children they're not intelligent, or that they will not achieve certain milestones. They can also develop when a parent compares children by constantly telling one to be more like the other. Parents have an especially great ability to positively or negatively impact developing paradigms, and therefore the emotions, actions, efforts, goals, dreams, and lives of their children. Think about the impact both Hitler and Martin Luther King, Jr. had on the world; that may give you an appreciation for how incredible this responsibility really is.

GROWTH MINDSET ON INTELLIGENCE

According to Dweck, people with a growth mindset believe intelligence isn't fixed, but instead can be continuously developed based on the efforts of the individual. From this perspective, intelligence is a choice everyone can access. This creates a desire to learn and embrace challenges, to be persistent in the face of setbacks, and to never give up, since success is achievable based on effort. Individuals with this perspective are not jealous of the success of others, but instead say, "If he or she can do it, so can I." They speak with people about how they overcame setbacks and achieved success. Basically, they are continuously expanding their paradigm and finding ways to manifest their idea of success. To me, a growth mindset means the person has some awareness of the power of their paradigms and uses that power for advancement.

Whether a person is intelligent or not is a fundamental characteristic that has vital implications for that person's future in our society. After all, what separates us from apes, according to Darwin, is intelligence, and thus it is a societal screening or measuring tool; however, I believe Dweck's work is much more meaningful and applies to not only intelligence, talents, or abilities but to any belief or paradigm we have. We can have a fixed mindset or paradigm about any topic, just like we can have a growth mindset about it. For anyone with a stuck paradigm, power lies in the ability to shift from a fixed to a growth paradigm.

I'm explicitly using paradigm versus mindset here because, as I mentioned earlier, I believe that mindset is outward looking, where a paradigm is the internal infrastructure created by the summation of our collective experiences and interactions up to that point. As a result, to shift a fixed paradigm, we need to be open about our limiting beliefs and willing to explore them. This can be done by reflection, dialogue, or experimentation.

Let's see how this can be done by using a personal example. My daughter, able to have full conversations at age two and undoubtedly a brilliant person, had difficulty with math in the second grade. At one point, she came to me and just couldn't figure out how to do the work, so she said, "I'm not good in math." I'm not sure where she heard this, but her current difficulty equated to her being no good in the subject. Well, to me that was a challenge to prove she could be as good as she wanted to; it was just a choice. If I allowed her to think that way, she could get stuck in that paradigm. Knowing how detrimental that could be, the proactive parent in me came out.

My first approach was explaining to her that math isn't intuitive. Math is like a language, and it would require her to memorize a lot of things. Eventually it would seem simple and make a lot more sense than it did now. I also explained to her that being good at anything was simply a choice to be good and to spend time practicing. I sat with her and explained how to do the problem in a step-by-step process with all the patience in the world. After she got that the problem at hand was a formula, she solved it over and over again. At first, it was me telling her she could do it, then after she did it, she said it to herself, demonstrating the success of the process via her own self-reflection. My aim was to create a growth mindset for my daughter in relation to math, which I believe I succeeded at, but I had to repeat this process many, many times.

Now let's imagine I didn't have any knowledge of paradigms or the importance of empowering her and that my approach was different. I could've just told her not everyone is good in math or math is hard, or I could have just done it for her. None of those actions would have allowed her to believe she was capable of doing math. Now imagine this process being repeated over and over again—my daughter would continue to believe she was not good in math.

This simple illustration shows how a fixed or growth mindset can be created for someone believing they're good in math or another subject, but it's applicable to pretty much any topic. In most situations, the majority of dialogue will be self-reflections, especially if the person is an adult, and require the individual to believe in themselves.

Fixed or growth mindsets are created from experience and dialogue. Thus, in order to create a growth mindset in any topic, believe you have the ability to achieve whatever the task or mission is and do not stop until you do so. Use a combination of continuous trial, error, and dialogue with yourself and others to make small improvements. As long as you don't give up, I guarantee you will succeed. Start with one issue and then tackle others one by one so you can understand how truly unstoppable you are. Eventually, you'll have a process by which to go from a stuck paradigm to a growth paradigm in any topic.

This proactive effort allows us to expand our paradigms, and, if necessary, eventually shift to a greater state of self-awareness. Using this method, you'll be able to do what you believed was impossible. Now imagine how difficult this is when changing the view of society for a specific topic.

A PURPOSEFUL PARADIGM SHIFT

As a result of the negative financial consequences of COVID-19, Stanford University decided to eliminate eleven sports teams from its offerings, including its 104-year-old wrestling program. Approximately 240 athletes from fencing, field hockey, lightweight rowing, rowing, sailing, squash, synchronized swimming, volleyball, and wrestling were going to be without a team. All the teams met this decision with fierce resistance. Two launched lawsuits against the institution, making two main arguments: misrepresentations (students selected Stanford because of the sport) and discrimination (female sports would be more impacted).

Members of the wrestling team, alumni, and supporters took a different approach. They founded the *Keep Stanford Wrestling* resistance movement. The key representative of the resistance was Shane Griffith, an exceptional wrestler who decided to try to win an NCAA Division One title to demonstrate the importance of the program in hopes of saving it. He would be only the second Division One title holder for the school. The win would be incredible branding for the program.

Griffith was a sophomore with numerous titles already under his belt. As a student at Bergen Catholic High School in New Jersey, he won multiple awards, including three state championships. As a freshman at Stanford, he was named the Amateur Wrestling News Rookie of the Year for his impressive undefeated first season (28-0). He also attained several tournament wins, such as Battle at the Citadel, the Roadrunner Open, and the Southern Scuffle (Scekic, 2020).

Despite an abridged season, he had the seventh-most wins by a freshman in team history. His twenty-eight consecutive wins were the second longest streak in the history of the wrestling program. Griffith earned a Pac-12 Championship in the 165-pound weight class in early March to be seeded number three in the NCAA Tournament before the championship was canceled due to COVID-19 in 2020 (Scekic, 2020).

"Devoting six months of training and sacrifice for one goal, and not even [being] able to try and obtain that goal, was hard," Griffith said to *The Stanford Daily*. "This circumstance always makes me think, 'Prepare for the worst, but expect the best.' There are always going to be bumps in the road,

but how you prevail is what truly makes you who you are"
(Scekic, 2020). These were wise words from a focused and
self-aware youth.

He even considered not participating in 2021 but decided
to use Stanford's decision to cut the program as motivation
to wrestle (Falk, 2021). "Obviously, just want to make this
[movement] nationally known, hopefully get it overturned.
We got a lot of young guys staying, trying to fight the battle"
(Bumbaca, 2021).

While he had wrestled for himself in the past, this journey
had deeper meaning. It would impact many other people
based on the multiplier effect if the entire program was saved.
This paradigm shift put more pressure on him to win. It also
really helped that he already had a growth mindset: "I like to
be pretty determined and shoot for the moon" (Anon, 2021).

The team wore black without Stanford logos and "Keep
Stanford Wrestling" on their sweatshirts during the NCAA
championships on March 21, 2021 to show displeasure for
Stanford's planned cuts. The journey was not easy. Griffith
was an eighth seed since he lost a match in the Pac-12 finals,
but he remained focused and undeterred. For each of the
three matches prior to the championship, he was tied in the
third period. He was victorious against Jake Wentzel from
Pittsburgh University in his final match to bring home the
Division One title in the 165-pound weight class (Anon, 2021).

To enhance the win, Keep Stanford Wrestling raised $12.4
million for the wrestling program, which posted a message
on their website after Stanford decided not to cut the team:

"To say this was a team effort would be the understatement of the century. Literally thousands of people stepped up in meaningful ways, large and small. Incredible humans drew on their time, their talents, their relationships, and their bank accounts to make today possible. Our coaches and wrestlers (and their parents) persevered through unimaginable circumstances to salvage what would become a historic season. And Shane Griffith put our message on his chest and our mission on his back for the whole world to see" (*Keep Stanford Wrestling*, 2021).

Their success was also a paradigm shift for the school, as Stanford decided not to cut any teams after Griffith's success and the collective support of all involved:

"We have new optimism based on new circumstances, including vigorous and broad-based philanthropic interest in Stanford Athletics on the part of our alumni, which have convinced us that raising the increased funds necessary to support all thirty-six of our varsity teams is an approach that can succeed," university president Marc Tessier-Lavigne said in a recent statement (Banagura, 2021).

Shane Griffith is a great example of the benefits of a growth mindset and the potential for operating with an expanded paradigm. He wasn't held back by limiting beliefs and used the benefits of his efforts to motivate himself to manifest his idea of success. His paradigm made him unstoppable.

SO WHAT DOES THIS MEAN FOR YOUR PARADIGM?

Research shows the key to resilience is optimism, which means a growth mindset—the belief you have the ability to positively impact your circumstances based on your efforts. I believe those with the paradigm of a growth mindset are unstoppable and capable of manifesting any goal they set out to execute.

Principle 5: Always have a positive outlook with a growth mindset and make lemonade from lemons. Be unstoppable in the face of challenges! You are more resilient than you think.

CHAPTER 6

Carpe Diem: Empower Your Reflection and Conversations

"No matter what anybody tells you, words
and ideas can change the world."

—JOHN KEATING (DEAD POETS SOCIETY, 1989)

The 1989 movie *Dead Poet's Society* is a great example of the power of reflection, conversation, and vulnerability, as well as the implications of facing or giving in to your fears.

The prestigious Welton Academy represents a societal paradigm reflecting the status quo—the prioritization of success and materialism over self-awareness, meaning, and purpose. Mr. Keating, a new teacher, offers a paradigm shift by inspiring students to develop self-awareness and a growth mindset. He is a breath of fresh air in contrast to the traditional, pompous teachers who "know everything" and have "fixed mindsets" and control the school.

Mr. Keating encourages students to "seize the day" and question their beliefs and the beliefs of others. He is intent on teaching them to "swim against the stream" and maintain their own beliefs, even when difficult, if others have strong opposing opinions. He acknowledges that humans have a need to be accepted by society and being unique may lead to unfavorable judgments, but he wants them to know there is power in authenticity. They will find themselves via their own unique voices.

To illustrate this point, he tells them to stand on their desks and see how different the world looks from up there. When reading poetry or verse, he encourages them to pay closer attention to what they themselves think rather than what the author suggests they ponder upon. He even has students rip out a section of a book telling them what should be considered good poetry, since appreciation of the same should be a personal preference and not defined by the preferences of one writer. He urges them to "dare to strike out and find new ground."

Mr. Keating's mind-opening perspectives have a significant impact on students and draws the ire of the school. In a quest to live more passionately, some students revive The Dead Poets' Society, a secret club inspired by Keating where they read poetry and verse and "suck the marrow out of life." But there are negative and positive consequences to living life more honestly. One student named Todd begins to understand the power of his voice and starts coming out of his shell, while another, Neil, decides to play a starring role in a town rendition of Shakespeare's *A Midsummer Night's Dream* against his father's wishes.

Mr. Keating dares students to reflect and expand their paradigms instead of numbly following the reality created by school and life officials. They should live authentic, passionate lives based on truth.

Unfortunately, Neil's father finds out about the play and pulls him out of school. His only sight is on his son attending Harvard, and distractions will not be permitted. Though Neil attempts to express his feelings, his father is not open to discussion and Neil gives up. Due to his trapped paradigm, he commits suicide, believing his dream of becoming an actor will never be allowed by his authoritative father.

Made the school's scapegoat for Neil's death, Mr. Keating is fired and goes to his class to pick up his belongings while the principal is teaching his old English course. Todd finds his courage and voice by standing on the desk prior to Mr. Keating leaving, demonstrating that he's now a free thinker, willing to face his fears (of punishment and public speaking) to live a passionate and authentic life. Other students follow his lead and the majority stand on their desks as transformed free thinkers paying homage to a great mentor who changed their lives. The principal screams at them to get down, but they don't care. They've found themselves and their power thanks to Mr. Keating, who smiles at them and leaves triumphantly!

YOUR PARADIGM IS A COMPLEX "SYSTEM"

Human bodies, companies, societies, cultures, and many other complex collections of processes are systems. Your paradigm is also a system (a subsystem of your body). Donella Meadows, a professor at Dartmouth College who was an expert on the topic, defined a system as "a group of connected elements with a shared purpose." In her book, *Thinking in Systems: A Primer*, she says every sustainable system relies on some kind of feedback for stabilization. For humans, I believe feedback is provided by ourselves via self-dialogue or by others via conversations—both are essential.

SINGLE VS. DOUBLE-LOOP LEARNING

Double-loop learning is an organizational concept developed by Chris Argyris, a business theorist and professor at Harvard Business School, in the 1980s. We can use this promising system to become aware of, cultivate, expand, and shift our paradigms. It relies on continuous communication loops that, if we chose to involve rational System Two processes, result in substantial learning and advancement.

As Shannon Cartwright described in her article "Double-Loop Learning: A Concept and Process for Leadership Educators" in the *Journal of Leadership Education*, "Double-loop learning is an educational concept and process that involves teaching people to think more deeply about their own assumptions and beliefs [. . .]. [It] is different than single-loop learning which involves changing methods and improving efficiency to obtain established objectives (i.e., 'doing things right'). Double-loop learning concerns changing the objectives themselves (i.e., 'doing the right things')."

This is what Argyris' double-loop process looks like in visual form, adapted for paradigms:

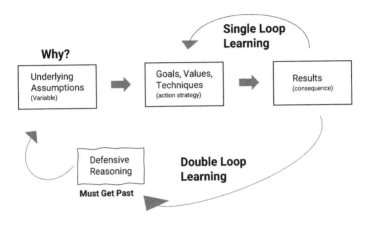

Chris Argyris used a simple thermostat analogy to describe how the process works: "A thermostat that automatically turns on the heat whenever the temperature in a room drops below sixty-eight degrees is a good example of single-loop learning. A thermostat that could ask, 'Why am I set at sixty-eight degrees?' and then explore whether or not some other temperature might more economically achieve the goal of heating the room would be engaging in double-loop learning" (Argyris, 1991).

The purpose of this book is to provide you with double-loop learning about your paradigm by bringing awareness and a system of circumvention to your fears, biases, and other processes keeping you in automatic, subconscious mode, robbing you of your full potential. The result is extensive self-awareness and personal power to manifest your definition of system.

What's interesting about the single vs. double-loop concepts is they're quite similar to Daniel Kahneman's System One (single-loop) and System Two Processes (double-loop). If we also consider how Helen Keller's paradigm was awakened via language and words, we can understand how essential the loops are to paradigm formation and growth. Despite having all mental functions, lack of language prevented her from being fully self-aware since she was not able to properly connect with others. She operated under System One single-loops prior to being taught how to communicate by Sullivan. Language and conversations led to the required system looping that enable consciousnesses, complex reasoning, and self-awareness.

Furthermore, looking at these processes from Brené Brown's vulnerability context explains the essential nature of the loops for human connections and paradigm formation, expansion, and shifting. Paradigms use System One systems and get stuck because the loop is automatic, irrational, and controlled by past experiences and biases. If we don't share vulnerably or authentically, the paradigm can also get stuck because the single loop just repeats itself automatically, with the wrong inputs, leading to undesired results. It requires a proactive System Two loop, aware and rational, to circumvent defensive reasoning—fear-based motives, biases, trauma, and other issues—to get unstuck via communication leading to a new way of thinking or understanding (i.e. Kuhn's paradigm crisis leads to a shift).

I believe this process of looping communication created the value of relationships demonstrated in the Harvard University Study of Adult Development, which we will discuss in chapter eleven. We truly open up to close friends and family in an aware, rational way that allows us to solve problems and gain self-awareness. Unfortunately, Neil didn't have this opportunity because he refused to open up to either his dad or Mr. Keating—he couldn't get past defensive reasoning—and his paradigm was stuck in a hopeless System One single-loop: the belief that his father would never allow him to become an actor. On the other hand, despite numerous defensive reasons, Will Hunting used a System Two double-loop to shift his paradigm because he was forced to be vulnerable by both Dr. Maguire and Skylar. Likewise, Todd faced his fear, passing defensive reasoning, to defend Mr. Keating because he believed he was unjustly blamed for Neil's death.

For paradigms, I see defensive reasoning manifesting as fear based on past experiences (or limiting beliefs). "But effective double-loop learning is not simply a function of how people feel. It is a reflection of how they think—that is, the cognitive rules or reasoning they use to design and implement their actions. Think of these rules as a kind of 'master program' stored in the brain, governing all behavior. Defensive reasoning can block learning even when the individual commitment to it is high, just as a computer program with hidden bugs can produce results exactly the opposite of what its designers had planned."

Argyris says that "in particular, they must learn how the very way they go about defining and solving problems can be a source of problems in its own right." But choosing self-awareness is a prerequisite to his deep insight and way of living.

According to Cartwright, "the strategy or method used to achieve this type of deeper learning is a form of communication, of dialogue that involves a good deal of interaction among learners. It proposes that the educator 'drill down' into a topic in order to identify and bring the taken-for-granted assumptions and beliefs of the learners to the surface. Double-Loop Learning helps people acquire and integrate new information and develop new skills, to question and possibly discard familiar and perhaps dysfunctional ways of thinking, feeling, and acting." She is talking about the teacher-to-student relationship here, but this also happens in everyday discussions with your friends as long as you are willing and able to open up.

"The usefulness of the strategy of double-loop learning for leadership education and development comes from its potential to extract tacit knowledge from individuals and convert it to explicit knowledge. It is a way to better understand the ordinary, to question our everyday working world, to think outside the presumptions and limitations that we have, perhaps unconsciously, constructed for ourselves" (Cartwright, 2021). This sounds very much like what Mr. Keating helped his students do by questioning theirs and others' beliefs!

In a sense, double-loop learning is similar to Kuhn's five-step paradigm cycle theory. Using double-loop learning, the normal paradigm experiences an anomaly, then a crisis which eventually shifts into a new and better way of seeing the world. We've all experienced deep, vulnerable discussions that caused us to see life differently and opened our eyes to new possibilities. That's double-loop learning.

REFLECTION AND CONVERSATION ENABLE THE
LOOPS THAT CREATE SELF-AWARENESS

To understand your life and seize the day, you need to understand the processes that can most empower you. The continuous learning that occurs with reflection and conversation are the loops to your system resulting in understanding, paradigm expansion, and self-awareness. The two comprise an elegant dance that, if care is taken to ensure coordination and processing, allows your paradigm to reach incredible heights.

Words—whether mental or spoken—to yourself or to others are the source of your power! In fact, they're the source of all human power, everywhere. There are no paradigms, no reality, no feelings, no knowledge, and no future without words. They're the means of communication that allow for human connection and coordination to create the world and all of its parts. We see communication as external, but it always loops back into our paradigms and our perception and understanding of reality increases as we reflect on what is discussed.

> *"Handle them carefully, for words have*
> *more power than atom bombs."*
>
> —PEARL STRACHAN HURD

Because we're not physically connected nor can we read the minds of other humans, we live most of our lives in our minds with ourselves. In this sense, we are born and will die alone. The only time we're not mentally alone is when we engage in conversation with another human being and truly listen. This is likely why human connection is so crucial to our being. Every other second of your life, you're in your head—thinking, making assumptions, creating meanings, being judgmental, planning, dreaming, and executing other internal processes that occupy your thoughts.

We likely spend over 95 percent of our existence alone in our thoughts and, for most of us, on autopilot. Besides these mental programs running in the background, there are two primary actions you may decide to take that will most critically shape your paradigms, your decisions, and your life: self-dialogue and discussions with others. Both of these can be System Two double-loops if vulnerability and self-awareness are involved.

> *"All I need is a sheet of paper and something to write with, and then I can turn the world upside down."*

—FRIEDRICH NIETZSCHE

SELF-DIALOGUE AND REFLECTION

Proactive reflection or self-dialogue is when you have an open, honest, and productive conversation with yourself to process an experience, a discussion, or other matters of importance to you, thereby occupying space in your mind. This mental process is purposeful and active and is distinct from when you're on autopilot mode and simply being reactive and not taking the time to process experiences, discussions, or ideas. We simply refer to it as "thinking" or "reflecting."

Since you are the engineer of your brain, this is when you write your proactive mental code or programming. From here, your creativity, desires, emotions, and goals arise. This is also the source of mental conflicts, which are a sure sign of Kuhn's crisis mode that can shift to System Two double-loops.

According to Jennifer Porter in her *Harvard Business Review* article, "Why You Should Make Time for Self-Reflection (Even If You Hate Doing It)," "at its simplest, reflection is about careful thought. But the kind of reflection that is really valuable to leaders is more nuanced than that. The most useful reflection involves the conscious consideration and analysis of beliefs and actions for the purpose of learning. Reflection gives the brain an opportunity to pause amidst the chaos, untangle and sort through observations and experiences, consider multiple possible interpretations, and create meaning. This meaning becomes learning, which can then inform future mindsets and actions. For leaders, this 'meaning making' is crucial to their ongoing growth and development."

Based on this insightful description, reflection expands your paradigms based on the looping that happens with proactive contemplation. Growth and development are created with the continuous loops of reflection, listening, and/or discussion.

Do you take time to reflect on your experiences and conversations to maximize your learning and self-awareness often?

Reflection is a crucial part of paradigm development. You can literally expand your paradigm by taking time to reflect, do mindfulness exercises, or just process any experience or conversation. A person who doesn't reflect will have a narrow paradigm and not live in true reality. As an example, imagine you're so busy at work that you have been working ninety hours a week for months and have been too busy to reflect and balance life. How would you feel? How would your paradigm be impacted? Would your relationships suffer?

Yes. You would be moody, quick to anger, and burnt out after some time. Your decision-making capabilities would be diminished. Your relationships would be negatively impacted. The lack of reflection means living a more stressful and less meaningful reality. It impacts your feelings and your happiness. Since you would be working ninety hours a week, you would have conversations all the time with colleagues, but no time to process many of them.

Poor reflection leads to poor decisions, since they're based on insufficiently processed information. This is especially important today, when we can literally occupy our minds constantly with social media, television, computers, and other technology. Taking time to reflect can literally be the difference between success and failure or happiness and misery.

However, reflecting isn't a passive activity and doesn't need to be done sitting down. It naturally occurs when you jog, exercise, read a book, and engage in other activities that do not require constant mental use. While everyone has the ability to reflect, most of us don't appreciate how important the process is. We don't prioritize doing it properly and sufficiently. Reflection may be as beneficial or *more* beneficial for our physical and mental health as sleep. I believe the recent popularity of mindfulness is directly correlated with the fact that we engage in less reflection based on the numerous distractions of today.

Insufficient reflection can also lead to the creation of limiting beliefs. If we don't take the time to adequately process an experience or a discussion, we may assume something was a mistake or our fault instead of gaining the holistic understanding brought about by an expanded paradigm. Just because you did not reflect, even if the outcome was positive, your mind will still use the experience for its System One autopilot mode, creating a problematic cycle on the basis of an unprocessed or poorly understood experience. You'll suffer the consequences of poor reflection in the future when you operate subconsciously, which you do 98 percent of the time.

While Neil initially spoke with Mr. Keating about his dad's demand to drop the play in *Dead Poet's Society*, his belief that he wouldn't agree limited his reflection and interaction. Neil chose to lie to Mr. Keating by telling him his father had agreed, rather than having another discussion on the matter.

He was so afraid of the outcome that he didn't dare to speak with his mother or others about it, trapping his paradigm in a state of unreality. Neil's father no doubt believed only he knew what was in the best interest of his son, but we can imagine how a strong confrontation from Neil, that no doubt would have shaken up the relationship in the short term, would have led to a stronger relationship in the future, or at least Neil chasing his dreams and finding the power of his own voice.

Another example of the power of reflection is failure. A failure can be converted into strong learning if the person takes the time to truly and honestly reflect on what went wrong, so as to be better prepared for future opportunities.

If you do not feel like you have much experience, reflection can seem difficult, especially at first. However, reflection can be made less cognitively demanding and more targeted through practice. There really are two ways of reflection. One is automatically noticing that one's automated responses aren't producing the expected result. The other is a broader sitting back and reflecting on how things are working overall. Good organizations do some of the latter when they have "lessons learned" discussions, so you may be more familiar and experienced with reflections that you think. You can do this on your own by thinking or writing down your own lessons learned.

THE POWER OF CONVERSATION—DIALOGUE MODE

Conversations are the doorway to vulnerability, expanded paradigms, and personal power. When someone feels listened to by you, they become more connected to you. Truly listening to someone is a necessity for vulnerability. It opens the door to connection because it shows the other person you care about what they have to say. You feel the same way when you're listened to as well. Conversation is the infrastructure that develops relationships with others and with yourself. Without them, paradigm growth is limited.

According to Sherry Turkle, the Abby Rockefeller Mauzé Professor of the Social Studies of Science and Technology at MIT and the founding director of the MIT Initiative on Technology and Self, "face to face conversation is the most human and humanizing thing we do." As she describes in her book *Reclaiming Conversation—The Power of Talk in a Digital Age*, "fully present to one another, we learn to listen. It is where we develop the capacity for empathy. It's where we experience the joy of being heard and of being understood.'"

In her book, Turkle also states that "conversation advances self-reflection, the conversations with ourselves that are the cornerstone of early development and continue throughout life." As she insinuates by that statement, when you talk to others, you talk to yourself as well. This is a really important point that most of us either don't know or don't focus on. Let's discuss a simple example to illustrate this critical fact.

Imagine you're in high school and you don't do your homework, but when your parents ask if you did, you say "yes." How big a deal is this in general? It seems like just a little white lie. You can do the homework in the morning and hand it in, no issues at all, right? Actually, while it appears to be a simple act with no real consequences, repercussions are in fact enormous. You have just written a code and a future System One heuristic short cut into your paradigm that will likely repeat and magnify.

The problem is you know you lied. Your parents may never know it, but the fact that you do means you're being inauthentic to yourself, an act that robs you of power. The most important person in life you have to trust is yourself, and when you tell lies, your ability to trust yourself diminishes.

Now you will consider yourself a liar, and a limited belief is created in your head that meaningfully impacts your paradigm and your power. Suffice it to say for now that any time you have a conversation and you lie, exaggerate, judge, complain, or say anything negative, you're listening to yourself, and it may be detrimentally limiting your paradigm.

So remember: when you talk to others, you're also listening! Your words about yourself will create self-judgments and limiting beliefs.

EFFECTIVE CONVERSATIONS SHAPE PARADIGMS AND LEAD TO CONNECTEDNESS

An effective conversation is comprised of a complicated mixture of internal and external elements—your entire paradigm, for example, including your willingness to be vulnerable—and experience sharing. Most of us are not taught how to think about conversations, so we learn by doing, sometimes incorrectly.

However, understanding and having a process for conversation is important for its effectiveness since it shapes our paradigm, emotions, and reality. There are two equally important aspects of effective conversation which lead to vulnerability. First, you must authentically and honestly share your thoughts, perspective, and experiences with the other person.

Then, you have to listen wholeheartedly without mental distractions or judgment and try to put yourself in that person's shoes as they speak.

Understanding Brené Brown's work on vulnerability, which we discussed in the previous chapter, is easy for us. It just makes sense. Practicing it, though, can be more complicated than logically agreeing it should be effective. Part of the complication is that when we listen to Brené Brown describe it in her TED Talk or read it in her book, it sounds like a simple, formulaic task.

However, the reality is we have to utilize emotions and our paradigms when we sit down to have a conversation with someone. This process is complicated and clouded by our pasts and the resulting fears and emotions. To further complicate this, we have very different feelings about specific people and they about us—we all have unique paradigms. As a result, conversations that may seem simple are extremely complicated processes which require us to be purposeful about them and to have an implementation strategy, particularly with people we care about.

Can you remember a time when you had to have a difficult discussion with someone and you dreaded it? Have you ever felt very upset when someone told you something and they didn't realize they hurt your feelings? What may seem like a simple comment to one person can be extremely hurtful to the other.

While Neil was able to sit down and be vulnerable with Mr. Keating, he wasn't able to find the courage to do so with his own father despite multiple attempts. His mental paradigm regarding his dad was full of fear, and it stopped him from communicating with devastating consequences.

Neil's relationship with his father is comprised of his father telling Neil what to do, and Neil attempting to express his desires but being too scared to do so. His father also never really allows Neil to express himself or talk back. When he does allow this, he's confrontational, as if to say, "Tell me what you have to say so that I can show you how you are wrong."

Neil didn't feel listened to by his father, and without that essential doorway to vulnerability, effective conversations are not possible. From each individual's perspective, the relationship was in a very distinct place. They both lived quite different realities that could have been connected and synced via truthful conversation.

As Yuhuda Berg said in her article "The Power of Your Words," published by *Thrive Global*, "Words are singularly the most powerful force available to humanity. We can choose to use this force constructively with words of encouragement, or destructively using words of despair. Words have energy and power with the ability to help, to heal, to hinder, to hurt, to harm, to humiliate, and to humble."

Since emotions are created or strengthened via effective conversations, the one-sided monologue by Neil's father was detrimental. As Turkle said, "To activate empathy, we need to create spaces where people can disagree on ideas while developing an understanding of other viewpoints [. . .]. We know that conversations are limited by our prejudices as much as by our distractions. Empathy doesn't begin with, 'I know how you feel.' It starts with the realization that you don't know how another feels. In that ignorance, you start with an offer of conversation."

This type of conversation, which would have been lifesaving for Neil, can only happen with a complete conversation in which both parties listen to each other and speak openly. However, it is important to note that Neil could have had the discussion with Mr. Keating, Todd, another friend, or any other person who would have genuinely listened to his perspective. He would have received significant paradigm expansion regardless of who the other person was.

These are some important questions that can help you improve your conversations:

- How do you view potential discussions?
- Are they opportunities to connect deeper with someone or an undesirable but necessary part of life?
- Think about what you share and ask yourself why you share that information.
- What information are you afraid to share?
- Who are you open and vulnerable with, and who are you uncomfortable speaking with? Why?
- Are there topics you ensure you do not bring up in conversations or shift the discussion away from if they do come up?
- When engaged in a conversation, do you really listen?
- Are you listening to respond or absorbing and processing what is being said?

- Do you mentally envision what the person is describing?
- How do you feel when you hear something you disagree with?

What I get most from Brené Brown's TED Talk is how important opening up and sharing vulnerably is for human connection. I also believe you have to listen vulnerably for connection to take place. According to William Ury in his TED Talk, *The Power of Listening,* "Listening is the missing half of communication. It is absolutely necessary but often overlooked." Ury says emotions depend on the power of listening and there are three key reasons to truly listen:

1. Listening to others helps us understand their paradigms.
2. Listening helps us connect with the other human being, helps us build rapport, and shows we care.
3. Listening makes it more likely that the other person will listen to us.

At a fundamental level, everybody wants to be heard and share their feelings, thoughts, and ideas. Ury says that "listening may be the golden key that opens the door to human relationships." He's right. According to Ury, "We often take listening for granted, as something easy and natural but in fact, real, genuine listening is something that needs to be practiced every day."

What William Ury is describing when he talks about genuine listening is not only hearing someone's words, but trying to understand their paradigm. "We listen from within their frame of reference, not only ours. We listen for what is behind the words. We listen to the underlying emotions and for what that person really needs and wants. We listen to their emotions, not only their words." It's easy to understand that the ending of *Dead Poet's Society* would have been quite different if Neil's father had done this.

Relationships fall apart when people stop listening to each other. The paradigms, which may have had a background of relatedness when the relationship commenced, expand differently and people say things like "we don't have anything in common anymore." It's more likely at some point the couple stopped genuinely listening, which then led to a discontinuation of vulnerably sharing with each other. This would in turn lead to the creation of limiting beliefs about the relationship, which, unless stopped, goes downhill from there. The answer is to see the paradigms from the couple as stuck, and to focus on collaborating to expand it with experience sharing and vulnerable discussions.

REFLECTION AND CONVERSATIONS CREATE MENTAL PROGRAMMING

From a biological perspective, both reflection and dialogue lead to the connection of neurons, the physical representation of your mental paradigm expansion. When you experience anything or have a conversation, you reflect and process it as well as create memories and emotions. Internally, your brain creates neuron connections to store those memories and emotions so you can access them later. Looking at it from this perspective, your paradigm has both a virtual as well as physical manifestation. As a result, what you feel, what you believe is reality, and what you believe as fact simply exist as neuron connections in your brain.

You create your reality. Just as no fingerprint is like another, no connection of brain neurons will be like any other. The richness of our unique experiences and paradigms gives meaning to life. Societal reality is created by the interaction, conversations, and words of humans. What this means is that without enough conversations with other humans, your reality will not be reflective of the collective, societal reality.

Do you live in the real world, or have you created your own reality? How can you determine which reality is right?

SO WHAT DOES THIS MEAN FOR YOUR PARADIGM?

To seize the day, create personal power, and add value to society, you must understand the importance of reflection and conversations as they literally write your mental codes and create your paradigms (physically and mentally). Both words and conversations are much more powerful than we realize, and they impact the people we speak with as well as ourselves. Our words and thoughts have power and create our reality and emotions, so we should be thoughtful about what we express and how we listen to ensure our paradigms reflect true reality.

Double-looping via conversation is critical because we can only see life from our own personal reality. When we engage in conversation, we're offered an ability to see life from someone else's paradigm and world view, which can inform our way of thinking, ideas, and perspectives. During conversation, we may disagree with the other person's perspective because it doesn't conform to how we see the world.

However, after a fruitful back and forth, we can realize we had a blind spot based on our past experiences, biases, or emotions that prevented understanding a specific perspective. To some people, if they're open and honest with themselves and can see through their biases, reflection may be enough to get to a new way of thinking. However, multiple discussions on topics with multiple people are likely to be a better, faster, and more efficient way to access true reality and understanding.

Realizing that conversations themselves require some reflection as to whether authenticity is possible given the circumstances is also important. Part of the paradigm needs to be knowing when to hold them and when to fold them in order to look for another conversational partner.

Principle 6: Engaging in thoughtful and proactive reflections and conversations are imperative aspects of effective paradigm cultivation.

CHAPTER 7

Do Not Be Controlled
by Your Emotions

"Assumptions are the termites of relationships."

—HENRY WINKLER

In *Pride and Prejudice*, the 1815 romantic satirical novel by Jane Austen, the protagonist, Elizabeth Bennet, learns a tough lesson about the repercussions of perfunctory assumptions and judgments that we can all benefit from. Her prejudice against Mr. Darcy leads to blinding emotions that nearly leave her and her family destitute.

The story is set in the English countryside at a time when marrying into wealth was one of the only ways of achieving status in society. More than two hundred years later, this story remains as popular as ever because we can all relate to being controlled and misguided by our emotions.

Darcy and Elizabeth meet at a ball where she overhears him tell his friend Mr. Bingley that "she is not pretty enough to temp [him]." This rejection is painful and informs her feelings for him, though they offer an incomplete picture. Darcy falls in love with her at another ball, but Elizabeth is blind to this fact—her lenses are clouded by her negative sentiments.

When Elizabeth learns Darcy is responsible for separating Mr. Bingley from her sister, she is outraged. Darcy's profession of ardent love for Elizabeth and his offer of marriage are rejected coldly and with utter contempt, despite the detrimental impact to her soon-to-be destitute family.

Elizabeth could never marry the person who gave eternal sadness to her sister. She informs Darcy that her sister is shy and barely shows her true feelings to anyone. Darcy had assumed Jane did not love Bingley and that the family was only after his fortune. On the basis of his unconfirmed assumptions, he separated two people who truly loved each other. However, Elizabeth thinks he did it because he believes Jane unworthy based of her lack of fortune.

Elizabeth judges the socially awkward Darcy as a proud, pompous, and inconsiderate man who only cares about money. Her assumptions are proved incorrect when Darcy reunites Jane and Bingley and saves her family by coordinating a wedding between a man and Elizabeth's silly young sister—they had eloped, an act that would have ruined the family if not for Darcy's rapid intervention and payment for their union.

When Darcy asks Elizabeth to marry him again, she accepts. She realizes her assumptions and judgments of him were incorrect, as were his prejudices about her and her family. Her expanded perception of him allows her to understand who he really is, and she falls in love with his true identity. The couples live happily ever after, and the Bennet family is saved from destitution not by one but two opportune and love-based weddings, a shift from the normal paradigm at the time.

THE PURPOSE OF EMOTIONS

Emotions are a powerful force in our lives, impacting our feelings, decision making, health (physical and mental), motivations, and most of human behavior. They're our constant companions. Our health and happiness literally depend on our emotions. While they generally run on autopilot, emotions are created by our paradigms and are under our control. However, most humans are not taught to control their emotions, so we grow up simply reacting to them, a habitual process leading to powerlessness and limiting beliefs.

As we saw in *Pride and Prejudice*, like most humans, Mr. Darcy and Elizabeth were controlled by their emotions and the basis for their decision making. This resulted in numerous misunderstandings, heartache, anger, disconnection, and all sorts of other unintended consequences. As humans, we assume our feelings are an accurate reflection of the world around us.

However, your emotions don't reflect reality! They're sensors intended to help you process the world, but we inadvertently interpret them as commands rather than alarms.

As we learned from chapter one, emotions are automatic System One processes and based on past experiences which could have been misinterpreted, incorrect, or a mistake. We therefore make decisions based on incorrect past information all the time.

Do you have a process or a system to explore and better understand your emotions? Most of us do not, as we aren't taught to do that—it requires self-awareness and effort. There's substantial power in proactively managing and understanding the purpose of your emotions.

YOUR EMOTIONS ARE NOT HARDWIRED— THEY ARE GUESSES

According to Dr. Lisa Feldman Barrett, University Distinguished Professor of Psychology and Director of the Interdisciplinary Affective Science Laboratory (IASLab) at Northeastern University, "Emotions are not hardwired brain reactions that are uncontrollable." She should know, as she has studied emotions in numerous ways and with over 1,000 human subjects for the past twenty years during her research appointments in the departments of psychiatry and radiology at Massachusetts General Hospital and Harvard Medical School.

During her TED Talk, Dr. Feldman says "the result of all of her research is overwhelmingly consistent. It may feel like your emotions are hardwired and that they just trigger and happen to you but they don't [. . .]. Emotions are guesses that your brain constructs where billions of brain cells are working together" and use your experiences and other information to make predictions. As a result, you have more control over those guesses than you think. "Emotions that seem to happen to you are actually made by you. If you change the ingredients you use to make the predictions, you can change your emotional life."

A change in the process of making emotions can expand our paradigms and unleash a great amount of personal power, regardless of the ingredients. The issue is we need to bring awareness to the process, study it, see what's working and what's not, and refine it. I, therefore, would take a more scientific approach to our emotion-making process to make sure we're not inadvertently creating bad emotions. The reality is that most of us do just that. We have an incomplete process leading to undesirable emotions, but that no longer has to be the case, as we will discuss below.

"The best way out is always through."

—ROBERT FROST

YOUR EMOTIONS ARE THE TIP OF THE ICEBERG

You've probably heard or used the phrase "the tip of the iceberg" at some point. The analogy is a powerful one when it comes to systems thinking and paradigms. Peter M. Senge, senior lecturer at the MIT Sloan School of Management and the founding chair of the Society for Organizational Learning (SOL), is the best-selling author of the book *The Fifth Discipline*. In this book, Senge popularized what is today known as The Iceberg Model for systems thinking.

I have adapted his popular general systems model to create a valuable tool to help you contextualize your emotions as part of a whole system (your paradigm), rather than an immediate representation of reality. Reality is the entire iceberg as well as how it relates to your paradigm (your past experiences, beliefs, etc.).

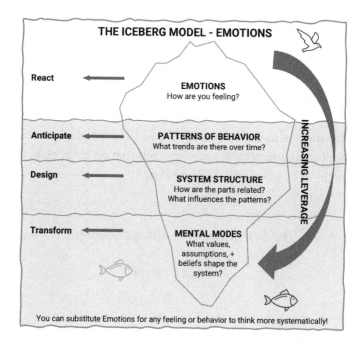

The key to properly using The Iceberg Model for emotions is connecting your emotion to patterns, behaviors, systems structures, and mental models, so you can understand the true source of that feeling and not be controlled by it. The model is very similar to double-loop learning but is more intuitive to some people because of the iceberg analogy. Just like an iceberg is 90 percent hidden under water, the source of your emotions is hidden in your paradigm. If you can identify the emotion and connect it to a past experience or memory, you may be able to develop long-term solutions targeting the entire system, versus a short-term reaction that's a band-aid on a serious injury if the emotion is negative.

Let's illustrate how this works with Brené Brown's vulnerability concept. The emotions causing disconnection are shame and fear, as we have already discussed. There's a definite pattern of behavior with these emotions. We repeatedly decide not to be vulnerable when presented with the opportunity to do so. Fear is the main pattern culprit here because of the shame it would create. As we saw in the last chapter, the real reason, which is part of our mental model, is we believe we're unworthy of love. We present an inauthentic version of ourselves we believe is more acceptable, which now creates more issues internally since we know we're lying to ourselves. If we're able to swim deeper and deeper into the iceberg and find and acknowledge the cause of the fear and shame, that feeling of "I'm not worthy," we can free ourselves up to vulnerability and shift our paradigm and our relationships.

THE EMOTION-MAKING PROCESS AND EMOTIONAL OUTPUTS

Emotions create our reality and point us in specific directions. They're a sensor or gauge meant to help us manage our lives, relationships, and reality; you have to understand there's a purpose to a human emotion before you have the ability to impact these things. Just like a car has sensors telling you when something is wrong or that you have to pay attention to a specific part of the car, emotions provide your brain information about how happy or sad you should be about your decisions or observations about life. Emotions are survival mechanisms meant to educate systems in your body. However, feelings only provide a glimpse based on a set of assumptions; you have to try to understand further to arrive at the source of the emotion. They're the tip of the iceberg.

ASSUMPTIONS

Humans are meaning-making machines, as many people in history have discovered. We are filled with curiosity and constantly make observations and assumptions about ourselves, others, and life. This is a normal part of human behavior, but it's not without risks. We should view an assumption as the beginning of a process that should be thoroughly completed for the best results.

Making assumptions about ourselves or others based on insufficient information leads to the creation of limiting beliefs and impacts our paradigms, emotions, and reality. Just like in *Pride and Prejudice*, if assumptions are hasty, they can lead us down an undesirable path. Thus, starting and fully completing this process is imperative. Remember, as Dr. Lisa Feldman Barrett discovered, emotions are predictions and you want to make the best guess possible, which is only doable with complete information.

This is what it looks like. You start to have a feeling based on a set of assumptions, and then you have a prediction to make. What do you do? Let's look at a simple example to demonstrate this point.

Erica, a twenty-one-year-old woman, started dating Ethan a couple of months ago. The relationship is going well, though they don't sufficiently know each other yet, adding to the excitement. At a friend's party during their second month together as a couple, Ethan is getting Erica a drink and appears to flirt with a beautiful woman who's also getting a drink. Erica immediately feels jealous and somewhat upset, but she knows she doesn't really know what is going on and her assumptions may not reflect reality.

What does she do? She can either conclude that Ethan was flirting based on her limited information, a conclusion that will undoubtedly have an impact on his current mood for the rest of the night, and their relationship, or she can ask for his side of the story and get the complete picture so she can inform that emotion. In most situations, the former would likely take place—but since we understand paradigms now, we know better. Saying nothing would not work, because she'd feel upset and would act on that emotion.

The example above would be a perfect time to use Brené Brown's advice to choose courage and use vulnerability to increase connectedness, though most people do the opposite. Having a proactive discussion about how Erica felt with her boyfriend would allow them to express assumptions and inform emotions. It would create a transparent process based on reality for both people to deal with this situation now and in the future. A relationship based on transparent discussions of the feelings of those involved will have a stronger foundation than one controlled by fear and unexplored assumptions.

Assumptions are a bifurcating road. One side leads to expanded paradigms, better relationships, and your true self. The other is controlled by fear and leads to miscommunication, disconnection, judgment, and weak relationships. Fear leads to unintended consequences and results in disconnection because we choose not to let people into our reality by being vulnerable.

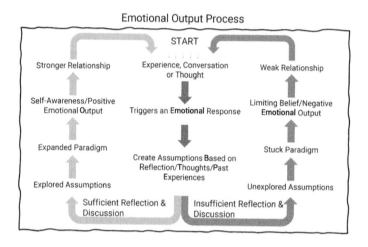

Assumptions are basically your internal version of a scientific hypothesis. In science, a hypothesis leads to additional research, exploration, experiments, greater understanding, and the creation of theory. Eventually, based on the exploration of many possibilities, a new theory can be created and cause a paradigm shift.

For humans, the same can be true if we take the curious path. As the famed American author Mark Twain stated on the topic, "It is wiser to find out than to suppose." The unexplored path leads to naivete, darkness, and a disconnection from reality. Instead of making an assumption a final conclusion, realize you don't have enough information. Go through the process of getting that information to inform your paradigm as a link to reality, greater self-awareness, and stronger relationships. If we realize this is a process and we continue to improve the method by seeking information, we'll become better at continuously expanding our paradigms and improving our relationships.

"Be a light, not a judge. Be a model, not a critic."

—STEPHEN R. COVEY

NEGATIVE EMOTIONAL OUTPUTS

Insufficiently considered or discussed assumptions lead to negative emotional outputs, such as judgments, complaints, grudges, jealousy, bitterness, hate, and many other negative feelings that detrimentally cloud reality and become part of how you filter the world. They are in fact more a reflection of your internal self than they are of your external reality. As Dr. Lisa Feldman Barrett pointed out, your emotions are guesses that take your past experiences into consideration (Barrett, 2017). You're creating an emotion based on your past experience to allow you to process a current reality.

Think of how much power and danger lies in that fact. It means that any experience offers you either wisdom or chains—you choose!

If you filter life through your past experiences, which most of us do, then your emotions are a look back to the past. Unresolved issues will make you a slave to your past emotions, whereas properly addressed issues will create wisdom leading to better relationships with yourself and others.

Most of us cannot let go of strong past emotions, so we're reliving mostly negative past experiences. This means most of us literally manifest the past in a continuous cyclical process if we have stuck paradigms. So much of how we see the world comes from our childhood and our parents. The difference between a loving home and a traumatic childhood will be with us and repeatedly pump emotions into our paradigms, clouding our reality, until we understand and expose the vicious cycle. All traumatic experiences which we find difficult to move on from allow those past emotions to control our present and future selves. Let's look at some negative emotional outputs typically holding us back, creating an alternative and murky reality.

JUDGMENTS

Judging someone creates a paradigm based on an incomplete set of assumptions from an inauthentic self. The reality is when you operate from your true, authentic self, you realize we're all struggling through our journey of life. Judgments are harsh and may create limiting beliefs for the person being judged. For example, if someone calls another person fat or dumb, they can leave a life-long mark if the party passing judgment is someone they love or if they already have insecurities. Judgments aren't based on reality but on a set of assumptions from the person fabricating them. Perhaps the person making the judgment was called fat or dumb at some point and they are just continuing a negative cycle.

What we don't realize is that judgments are highly damaging to the person making them as well, possibly even more so than for the one who is judged. Judgments are more reflective of the "I'm not good enough" paradigm of the speaker than they are of the person being described. A great example of this is a bible story from John's Gospel in the King James Bible, in which the Pharisees and scribes bring an adulterous woman to Jesus and ask Him to judge her.

The story is so powerful because it illustrates the potency of judgments. In Jesus' time, a judgment, whether true or false, could literally mean the stoning and death of the accused. What Jesus pointed out to these accusers was that they were all sinners as well and could also be judged and found guilty. As a matter of fact, they found themselves guilty, as demonstrated by their leaving after Jesus challenged those without sins to cast the first stone. They all left, one by one. Any of us who judges shall be judged internally by our paradigms and found guilty as well.

The point of the story is that we're all imperfect and make mistakes, like the woman who committed adultery. Casting judgment on others when we are guilty as well is hypocritical and doing so is inauthentic. While today we may not cause the stoning or killing of those we judge, we impact their paradigms and their reality, which also has detrimental consequences. We create undue hardship on another human.

Another important point we may miss is that we may be judging others because of the guilt and shame we feel about ourselves. We may be subconsciously reacting to how we feel about our own actions and resort to judging as a way to self-soothe and feel better about ourselves. When you judge, catch yourself and explore your paradigm, searching for the reason you're judging others. You'll find stuck paradigms leading to an inauthentic self. A judgment is an internal sensor pointing to unresolved issues that you need to deal with.

> *"Be Curious, Not Judgmental."*

—WALT WHITMAN

COMPLAINING

According to the Merriam-Webster dictionary, to complain is "to express grief, pain, or discontent." The occasional complaints from those who find fault infrequently are likely harmless, but a person who routinely complains is stuck in a specific mindset or paradigm and will not be set free until it's addressed. A complaint should also be viewed as a sensor indicating that something needs attention. The person complaining should stop and reflect about what the true issue at hand could be, since many times we complain without understanding the true cause. What's submerged below the tip of the iceberg?

We need to bring awareness to the stuck paradigm and expand it. From this perspective, a complaint is our subconscious informing us that a paradigm is in crisis. Complaints are isolated, continuous loops, like a thermostat being set to a specific temperature when the issue is not related to weather. The solution is to use Chris Argyris' double-loop learning system to understand and get past the issues. Complaining is the defensive reasoning Argyris spoke about, which prevents a double loop evaluating the underlying assumptions.

Utilizing the Emotional Output Process from above, the complaint is an emotional response to an experience, thought, or discussion that happened in the past. You may not fully understand the emotion yet but need to bring awareness via reflection. Once you bring awareness to it, you can process the feeling by thinking thoroughly about what happened. You should also speak with friends about your feelings to make sure you get diverse perspectives.

This will allow you to explore and expand the paradigm, leading to greater self-awareness and stronger relationships with yourself and others. Make sure to repeat this process every time you find yourself complaining about something. Complaining is a call to action if you want to keep your power and deal with the situation consciously. Constantly complaining about something or someone will lead to a state of powerlessness and negative emotional outputs such as anger, jealousy, bitterness, etc.

Complaints also impact your relationships. People appreciate a discussion regarding a complaint or feeling if you actively involve them in solving the problem. If you're vulnerable and they have an opportunity to connect deeper with you, it could be a fruitful conversation; however, complaining in a manner allowing you to vent with limited involvement from the other person in the conversation can actually disconnect you from them.

Oftentimes, we complain or make snappy comments when something is bothering us without even realizing it. Have you ever done that? I often catch myself doing this when I'm sleep deprived, anxious about something, tired, or when I'm thinking about an unpleasant experience or conversation. I've noticed that even a smell reminiscent of an undesirable past situation can create negative moods. We're complicated organisms with numerous automatic systems to be aware of and bring to the surface.

If someone brings a complaint to you in conversation, realize the complaint says a lot about how that person is feeling inside and try to help them, not judge them. Look within the complaint as it offers views of the person's paradigms. Try to experience share and briefly state a time when you were going through something similar. Then, ask probing questions and genuinely listen to their responses without interrupting. It may be a sign of a person on autopilot having a paradigm crisis.

This is an opportunity for you and another person to expand each other's paradigms. Something isn't working and they may not be sure what it is. You may be able to help them bring awareness to it so they can make conscious decisions to address the complaints and expand their paradigms. Remember, this isn't something taught to us, but since you now have greater awareness, you can make a difference in someone's life by helping them become more self-aware. However, be sensitive to the fact that they may not welcome your advice and watch for clues that they're open to the discussion.

Though you aren't at the mercy of your emotions, your goal should not be to control them. A better way to look at this process is that you want to understand your own emotions. You want to bring awareness to them and explore them so you're not enslaved and reliving them in a continuous, unconscious, and uncontrollable cycle.

A quick way to understand the power of this process is to think of a time when you felt anger toward someone. Remember the last time you were upset with your spouse, sibling, or best friend. They did something that hurt your feelings and you felt anger toward them. The feeling of anger controlled how you related to them, how you spoke with them, how you felt about them, and even how you saw the world.

Your reality toward them was clouded with negative feelings, which impacted everything else you did as well as your relationships with others. These feelings persisted until you had a discussion in which you were vulnerable and forgave that person. Thereafter, you were freed from those negative feelings and were happy with your loved one again.

Emotions color our entire world, but we don't have to be a slave to our feelings.

Shockingly, I know people who haven't spoken with a father, mother, or ex-spouse for over twenty years. Can you imagine the impact that stuck paradigm has on them both? Moreover, imagine the impact on their kids if they were married, or on their sibling if they were parents. There is a substantial multiplier effect on stuck paradigms permeating through ourselves and our relationships.

Now that you have awareness of the benefits to yourself by removing the chains of negative emotional outputs, consider reaching out to people for whom you feel negative emotions and have an honest, vulnerable discussion as a way to free yourself from those chains. You may create a stronger relationship with that person than you thought possible.

Imagine if you were able to free yourself from all the grudges, bitterness, jealousy, hate, and other negative emotions you feel. How would your perspective on life, your mood, and your purpose change? How much stronger would your relationship with yourself and others be?

What can you do right now to start freeing yourself from the chains of negative emotional outputs?

POSITIVE EMOTIONAL OUTPUTS

If assumptions and emotions are fully explored, they can lead to positive emotional outputs and allow us to acquire wisdom and stronger relationships with ourselves and others. Since we know from chapter two that fear and shame lead to a lack of vulnerability and limiting beliefs, let's explore the benefits to those with the courage to fully explore assumptions, judgments, and complaints—the wholehearted group of which Brené Brown spoke.

These people understand being vulnerable is risky because emotions expose them to heartache and pain, but they know they have to go through the entire process to be true to themselves and keep their power. On the other side of fully exploring their assumptions, they can find love, gratitude, appreciation, empathy, forgiveness, kindness, and selflessness. Like the proverbial pot of gold at the end of a rainbow, there is also tremendous self-awareness on the other side of vulnerability.

SO WHAT DOES THIS MEAN FOR YOUR PARADIGM?

Understanding our emotions is a journey and requires constant attention. We're emotional beings, after all. Choose to see emotions as doors to be opened so you can expand your paradigm and free yourself from limiting beliefs. Emotions are like sensors pointing to a problem.

We have to overcome the fear we may feel when that sensor is activated and face the emotions to overcome them and create a new paradigm. Not doing so will have detrimental consequences in our lives and relationships.

Principle 7: Emotions are sensors pointing to important feelings that need to be further explored. They are the tip of the iceberg and lead to greater self-awareness and personal power if addressed or result in stuck paradigms and limiting beliefs if ignored. They should be viewed as part of the decision-making process versus the entire reason from which to make decisions.

CHAPTER 8

Honor Your Word to Create an Authentic You

———

*"Being entirely honest with oneself
is a worthwhile endeavor."*

—SIGMUND FREUD

The Shawshank Redemption (1994) is a movie about an innocent man (Andy Dufresne) who, after getting convicted of
murdering his wife and her lover, is sent to Shawshank State
prison to serve two consecutive life sentences. The state of all
other prisoners can be summed up with a comment by Red,
a prisoner in jail for twenty years for murder: "These walls
are funny. First, you hate them, then you get used to them.
Enough time passes, gets so you depend on them." Guilty
or not, they give in to prisoner mentality, which is an inauthentic way of being. But as demonstrated by this comment,
Dufresne does not succumb to this stuck paradigm: "Hope
is a good thing, maybe the best of things, and no good thing
ever dies." Despite an environment full of people out of sync

with reality, he remains true to himself and plans an escape which takes twenty years to execute.

Through much risk and effort, he creates a post-prison reality that may be superior to the one he had prior to being incarcerated. From film critic Roger Ebert's perspective, the movie is "an allegory for maintaining one's feeling of self-worth when placed in a hopeless position" (Fandom, 2021). While I agree with him, the meaning of the movie is much deeper and very complicated.

The film is a powerful representation of how we imprison our minds by saying or committing acts against our principles, limiting our reality and power by giving into inauthenticity, and it demonstrates the significant amount of effort required to live an authentic life in sync with true reality. Most of us (represented by the prisoners in the movie) get stuck in personal realities that are the equivalent of mental incarceration. As we've learned from past chapters, only ten to fifteen out of one hundred people are really self-aware (Eurich, 2017). The rest of us live in autopilot mode, reacting subconsciously to life with little power. We don't see the paradigms in which we are imprisoned.

The main issue is that this happens slowly, and we don't know how we end up here if we even have awareness of the dilemma. Like the frog placed in a pot of water who does not realize the temperature is increasing slowly until it's too late, we live in broken paradigms. Red was one of the only people who understood this, demonstrated by his continuous effort to get parole and to free himself from that reality, as compared to the elderly man who was released and killed himself since he could not live in the real world.

Our prison is created via the words we use to process or describe experiences, feelings, and emotions. Little by little, our words lead to seemingly insignificant actions that eventually become impenetrable mental blocks, separating us from ourselves and from true reality.

LOCUS OF CONTROL

Julian Rotter, an American psychologist who was a professor at Ohio State University and University of Connecticut, is credited with creating Social Learning Theory and Locus of Control Theory. Social Learning Theory is similar to a self-fulfilling prophecy—if we expect something will happen and it does, then our expectation was fulfilled and vice versa (University of Virginia, 2021).

His Locus of Control Theory essentially states that individuals who believe their behavior is deterministic of outcomes and circumstances—meaning they can cause things to happen—possess an Internal Locus of Control. On the other hand, people who believe fate, chance, destiny, or other external factors are responsible for events have an External Locus of Control. You can think of Internal Locus of Control as similar to Carol Dweck's Growth Mindset whereas External Locus of Control would relate to having a Fixed Mindset.

Like people with a growth mindset, those who have internal locus of control believe the outcomes of their actions are results of their own abilities and decisions—hard work leads to positive outcomes (April et al, 2012).

According to research, successful leaders and high achievers have high internal locus of control, whereas less successful people have low internal locus of control (Hiers & Heckel, 1977; Anderson & Schneider, 1978; McCullough et al., 1994).

There is no doubt Andy Dufresne had an internal locus of control based on his proactive, methodical, and strategic success in escaping Shawshank State Prison. People willing and able to cultivate their paradigms and increase their self-awareness also fit that description.

I also believe the ability to honor your word is a major characteristic of having an internal locus of control which results in the substantial ability to manifest your definition of success.

THE MOST IMPORTANT LESSON
Perhaps the most important lesson my father taught me was to always honor my word. He did this both by encouraging me to do so and, more importantly, by doing it himself. If my father said he would do something, he always, always followed through, without exception. His word is his bond and he never compromises this trait. He also never over promises to make sure he can honor his commitments.

If I had to choose one personal trait that is most responsible for allowing me to transform myself from an impoverished immigrant to a Harvard Business School alum and successful entrepreneur, it would be consistency honoring my word—to myself and others. I've been able to manifest anything my mind thinks of based on this one trait, regardless of how easy or hard it may seem to others or how long it takes. This means I can trust myself 100 percent to honor my commitments. Looking back at my life, I can see how much power this trait has given me. It also substantially shaped my paradigms in positive ways and gave me access to real truth, versus the perceived truth that my mind can create.

Imagine you could say, "I'm going to lose fifteen pounds by a specific date" and know without a doubt you'd accomplish it. It sounds easy, right? You just have to do what you say you'll do. As we learned, the mind is clouded with fear and other emotions sidetracking us from our goals or what we know is right.

It took me a while to build this muscle, but eventually I got to the point where I could trust myself fully, which unleashed a tremendous amount of power for me. I would say or think I would do something, and I could take it to the bank because there was absolutely no doubt I would follow through. I allowed myself no exceptions. I could make any goal, structure my day in any way, or make any promise, and I would stick to it. There was nothing of greater priority than my word, so I wouldn't allow myself or anyone to change my plans.

For example, because exercise and health are important to me, when I got bored of weight training a few years ago, I said I would start jogging and run a half marathon. I learned what was required, trained properly, and honored my commitment to myself. When my knees started giving me issues, I stopped running and I said I would do 100 push-ups a day instead. For 180 days, without a single exception, I did them. It was only when my shoulders started giving me problems that I switched to Brazilian Jiu jitsu, an exercise I fell in love with and have been doing for years.

I also created goals for my grades in school since I wanted to attend the best academic institutions possible. I achieved them and got into every college I applied to and selected Cornell University. For my MBA, I decided to attend Harvard Business School, but I was also accepted at MIT, Columbia Business School, and the Cornell SC Johnson School of Business. These are great schools. I don't say this to brag—working on my paradigms and honoring my word allowed me to accomplish these impressive goals. As an ambitious planner, I have been able to accomplish goal after goal after goal to get to where I am today by simply honoring my word and doing what is required to follow through. You and anyone else can do the same!

As Ralph Waldo Emerson once said, "Self-trust is the first secret of success" and the only way to achieve self-trust is honoring your word!

HONOR YOUR WORD

Truly honoring your word means committing to following through with anything you say you will do 100 percent of the time. In a world where most of us walk around with stuck paradigms, in denial and numb to reality, those that honor their word consistently stick out like a sore thumb, as did Andy Dufresne. They are likely to be the ugly duckling in the family, described as taking themselves too seriously, not knowing how to have fun, and being too blunt or too honest, or perhaps even rude. That's certainly how I've been described at times, even by my loved ones.

Putting the judgments of those unable to honor their word aside, people who do so experience the world differently because they see true reality. They commit to seeing the truth inside and outside of themselves, which requires an exceptional amount of courage and hard work. It's a proactive decision. This mindset is developed one step at a time by ensuring words are honored consistently.

Doing this requires a mental muscle that must be developed on the basis of commitment and relentless effort. As a result, people who honor their word have a stronger grasp of reality based on a foundation of self-trust and an ardent refusal to live in denial.

When people speak about honoring their word, they usually speak about honoring commitments verbalized to other people. This is important, but not as important as honoring the commitments you make to yourself. If you don't trust yourself to do what you say or tell yourself you will do, you're most likely walking around with stuck paradigms that must be addressed— and we all have these. You likely don't fully understand what the internal issues are and should proactively address all or as many issues or limiting beliefs as possible as a way to empower yourself and be in sync with reality. This action will set you on the path to honor your word and trust yourself again.

Self-esteem, honor, integrity, authenticity, courage, dignity, love, commitment, and many other important attributes flow from consistently honoring your word. If you do this, you're able to be true to yourself. The essence of true, authentic power from true selves creates powerful paradigms.

The capacity to trust yourself is also the foundation for relationships with others, because once you trust yourself, others can also trust you. How much better would your relationships be if, when you told people you would do something, you always did?

How amazing would your *life* be if you were able to tell yourself that you would do something and you always did?

As is always the case, one single lack of following through can kill trust. This is the case in relationships with others and, especially, within your relationship with yourself. This is why I told the story of the little white lie in a previous chapter. If you doubt you'll actually do what you say you will, your life will be chaotic. We're all imperfect, and as a result, you have to forgive yourself if you mess up. We all do. But it's essential to hold yourself accountable. If you mess up, you must truly commit to do better next time and do your best to follow through. More importantly, commit to honoring your word 100 percent of the time and recommit fervently with every failure to do so. There are no exceptions to this rule.

CLAYTON CHRISTENSEN

Clayton Christensen is a great example of a business professional who was a larger-than-life figure based on his self-awareness, authenticity, and substantial impact on his loved ones and society.

He was the Kim B. Clark Professor of Business Administration at Harvard Business School, where he taught the Building and Sustaining a Successful Enterprise class—one of the most popular elective courses for second-year students (Christensen, 2021). In addition to eight other books and hundreds of articles, he was the author of *How Will You Measure Your Life*, where he makes candid observations and provides honest insights meant to help readers design personal paths to fulfillment.

In the book, he describes how many of the business lessons he learned and taught apply to human behavior as well as to business enterprises. This is something I fundamentally agree with and would argue also applies to science, as we saw with Kuhn's Five-Cycle Paradigm work on chapter two, Meadows' Systems Thinking, Argyris' Double-Loop Learning, and Seligman's Iceberg Model.

Communities of people in all disciplines have developed scientific and business methods highly applicable to our own lives that can help us improve. For example, I see Christensen's work on Disruptive Innovation—a term he coined describing a process by which a product or service takes root initially in simple applications at the bottom of a market and then relentlessly moves up market, eventually displacing established competitors—as the equivalent of paradigm crises leading to paradigm shifts for humans (Christensen, 2021). This is the business equivalent to Kuhn's paradigm cycle, also reflecting human behavior.

Though I was at Harvard Business School when Christensen was teaching there, I never had the privilege of taking his class or meeting him. However, I am convinced he fundamentally understood the paradigm framework I'm describing in this book, probably at a level significantly greater than most of us ever will. Whereas we create mental codes for ourselves, Christensen was like a master programmer teaching us the basics of business and personal paradigm creation.

Clayton Christensen wore many hats in his life, allowing him to have expanded paradigms and be in closer sync with true reality than most of us. Perhaps the most important characteristic that shaped his life was that he was deeply religious and a member of the Church of Jesus Christ of Latter-day Saints, also known as the Mormon Church. His religious beliefs and work allowed him to maintain an important perspective on life based on key morals, principles, and virtues. He had a strong sense of purpose and tried to make a difference to others in many ways, including missionary work and writing *How Will You Measure Your Life*. His goal was to positively impact his family, students, the business community, and the world.

"The church helps me understand and practice the essence of Christianity. The mechanism by which the organization achieves this is to have no professional clergy. We don't hire ministers or priests to teach and care for us. This forces us to teach and care for each other—and in my view, this is the core of Christian living as Christ taught it" (Christensen, 2021).

Deep religious faith can allow us to access reality and expand our paradigms in powerful ways. For Clayton, interactions with fellow church members and their missionary work in parts of the world in need provided a strong sense of purpose, which allowed him to balance his ego, expand his paradigms, and access reality.

Christensen had numerous roles that impacted his perspective, but teaching was likely the most important since it allowed observation, reflection, conversation, and diverse perspectives. As a professor, he taught large classes (normally ninety students) using the case method (Christensen, 2021). The HBS teaching method requires students to read a case where they view themselves as the protagonist, solving a key management problem. They reflect on the problem and then discuss it with classmates in and outside of class. The professor moderates student discussions, but it is up to them to find adequate solutions.

It usually becomes evident that numerous potential solutions exist, depending on the problem and their specific experiences, which they share. Students experience-share and continuously discuss the problem and its potential solutions. As alumni, they have a framework from which to resolve issues as they encounter them, making this teaching method superior to book learning, in my opinion, which is largely self-learning. This powerfully and effectively develops a specific paradigm for decision making.

I found the case method invaluable as a student at HBS. When I was a Hotel Administration major at Cornell University, I formed a solid foundation on business principles from studying textbooks and attending classes. A key reason I decided to attend HBS was that I wanted to study from a different perspective. The ability to thoroughly discuss and reflect on these topics with hundreds of other students during my two years there provided deeper understanding and built leadership muscles based on repetition. The experience created a meaningfully expanded leadership and management paradigm.

As a professor at HBS for twenty-eight years, hearing the perspectives of diverse students from all over the world and from all possible industries, Clayton Christensen had the ability to meaningfully expand his paradigm in a way most humans never can. As I witnessed during my time there, HBS professors are extremely disciplined and focused on continuous pedagogical improvement—if they don't receive tenure in seven years, they're out. They engage in frequent group discussions to improve their teaching methods and success, which provides a meaningful competitive advantage.

Teaching innovation and strategy at HBS allowed Christensen to view business strategy, leadership, and human behavior from a very unique and insightful perspective, especially when coupled with his efforts out of the classroom (like his religious work) and with his life experiences.

Prior to his academic career, Clayton worked as a management consultant with Boston Consulting Group (BCG). Management consultants work with clients to identify and solve complex business, organizational, and operational problems, and to define and improve processes (Allen, 2021). Clayton's experience exposed him to diverse firms, problems, and organizations.

After working at BCG, Christenson co-founded Ceramics Process Systems Corp, a Massachusetts-based advanced materials company. He subsequently helped establish many other successful enterprises, including the innovation consulting firm Innosight, the public policy think tank Innosight Institute, and the investment firm Rose Park Advisors. He was also active with the Boy Scouts of America for twenty-five years in numerous roles.

Looking at life from this rich combination of experiences as well as teaching life and business principles, it's no wonder that Christensen believed in the significance of always honoring your word. It was an important aspect of his life that allowed him to be authentic and connect with his true self.

As he described in *How Will You Measure Your Life*, Christensen believed that "the marginal cost of doing something 'just this once' (like telling a white lie) always seems negligible, but the full cost will typically be much higher." It was this same principle that convinced me to never make exceptions when I made goals. I knew it was a downhill slope thereafter. One exception would lead to another, then to another—to the destruction of the foundation of the principle and eventual corruption of honoring my word. As a result, I fully agree with Clay Christensen that honoring your word "100 percent of the time is easier than 98 percent of the time." Based on his amazing career and life, as well as his principled perspective, he understood this better than anyone.

In *The Shawshank Redemption*, all prisoners initially said they were innocent, regardless of their guilt. Eventually, most of them would admit their guilt, confirming they were lying to create fake, more lovable versions of themselves. Dufresne, however, was innocent and never relented on that or any truth. He remained authentic to himself the entire time he was imprisoned. He also didn't give in to the marginal thinking that doing something wrong one time was okay. As Christensen described, in any other area of life, marginal thinking is a downhill slope. He was authentic, tried his best, was selfless, and saw reality the entire time while other prisoners lived in chaos.

Christensen's marginal thinking rule applies to all areas of our lives, including but not limited to honoring our word, our virtues, and our principles, as well as trying our best in all that we do and other elements key for being our true selves.

Have you ever said, "just this one time" and remembered it was like crossing the Schwarzschild Radius of a blackhole—impossible to get out of the pull of the black hole the second, third, and fourth...x times? We all have!

The key is to eliminate *all* marginal thinking.

Are there any areas of your life where marginal thinking and the inability to honor your word or any other principle or virtue are limiting your potential?

THE POWER OF DECISIONS
A decision is a way to manifest the future by proactively planning to do something. Decision making is an internal process depending heavily on all other past choices, feelings, reflections, conversations, and experiences. Your current mental algorithm, which you created throughout your life, produces

this internal process. It flows from your paradigm and is like a calculator, except exponentially more complicated.

Once a decision is made, it depends heavily on your ability to honor your word.

The power of decision making relies on your paradigms and your word. If you make decisions and don't have the ability to follow through, you will be like a gun shooting blanks. How useful is that gun on the battlefield? How useful would the ability to make decisions and not follow through be in the battlefield of your life, your relationships, and your career? As we discussed above, the inability to honor your word may signify the existence of stuck paradigms requiring attention.

Here is what that reality would look like as a formula:

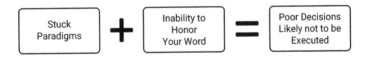

The ability to manifest your idea of success under this situation would be limited. You may know what you want and decide to go after it, but it wouldn't work because you wouldn't honor your word. Your stuck paradigms and all the drama created as a result cloud your judgments, bring out your limiting beliefs, and take your power. Even if you get to the point where you are in a position to execute decisions, they would not be productive.

What would the situation look like if you had expanded paradigms and the ability to honor your word?

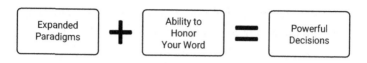

From this perspective, you'd be able to make decisions, honor your word, and make your goals a reality. Regardless of your background, the color of your skin, your socioeconomic situation, or any other factor, a person operating from this level would be unstoppable.

Since he was innocent and unjustly incarcerated for the rest of his life, Andy Dufresne made a decision shortly after arriving at Shawshank State Prison. He decided to escape, which was his definition of success based on his situation. He was innocent and unjustly incarcerated. He knew it was no easy task and it would take patience, perseverance, focus, and the (unknowing) participation of others at the jail.

He used a tiny hammer, secured from a friend with access to restricted items, and gradually scraped and chipped his way through the wall over a twenty-year period. He hid his work behind a large poster. His favors to prison guards and the warden resulted in special treatment, like keeping the poster, and other benefits enabling his goals.

Despite both the chaos and powerlessness of prison life for every other prisoner, Andy succeeded when others failed due to expanded paradigms and by honoring his word (to himself) to escape. He also found a way to rid the jail of the evil warden and his crew, substantially improving life for the rest of the inmates. He added meaningful value to his society while every other prisoner worried solely about his own situation.

What could you achieved in five years, ten years, twenty years, or in your entire life if you had expanded paradigms and the ability to honor your word?

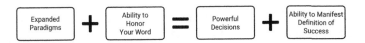

Perhaps the better question is what *couldn't* you do? When I decided to make education my roadway to my definition of success, it required chipping away at every homework assignment, every test, and every class for over a decade until I came out on the other side with undergraduate and graduate degrees. It required prioritizing education over many tempting options. I never gave in to marginal thinking.

Sure, there were chaotic times, but I kept my power by honoring my word, allowing me to succeed. I was committed to my goal, and I had the right frame of mind to make it happen. I was relentless and focused on it. No matter what anyone said (my HS school counselor or any of the many naysayers I encountered), I told myself I would succeed. I never doubted myself because I trusted my ability to honor my word. I knew it was a matter of focus and effort. I was playing the long game.

I had the power and so do you!

SO WHAT DOES THIS MEAN FOR YOUR PARADIGM?

Our paradigms have a direct impact on our ability to honor our word and follow through on our decisions. Our lives are essentially a collection or sum of our decisions, therefore it is imperative to manifest your definition of success, to decide what your definition of success is as early on in life as possible, and to set out to execute it. The most powerful weapon you have to execute your goals is your word and the ability to stay focused for the long term, as Dufresne did, in the face of a world full of inauthentic people who do not care about honoring commitments they make to themselves and others.

If you don't know where you're going, you'll never get there. An expanded paradigm coupled with the ability to honor your word allows you to achieve your definition of success regardless of your birth or current circumstances.

Principle 8: The ability to honor your word to yourself and others is not easy, but it's an essential muscle that must be strengthened for you to find your true, authentic self, increase self-awareness, and manifest your definition of success via effective decision making.

CHAPTER 9

Develop Your True Self to Access Reality

———

*"Be who you were created to be, and
you will set the world on fire."*

—ST. CATHERINE OF SIENNA

How does Mahatma Gandhi, a simple and common man,
become one of the most impactful human beings ever to walk
planet Earth and perhaps its greatest example of authentic
leadership? What was so special about this feeble-looking
man that allowed him to take on and lead a defeat of the powerful British rule by inspiring millions of his fellow citizens?

Absolutely nothing—at first, that is!

He wasn't born with any remarkable abilities allowing anyone
at the time to foretell of the historic giant we envision when
someone utters the name "Gandhi." It was the empowerment

manifested by a carefully cultivated set of principles which we've already discussed in this book. These are self-awareness, vulnerability, a growth mindset, resilience, and morality, which enabled him to develop a powerful paradigm, deeply connected to reality via a lifelong trial-and-error process. It seems few of us achieve that milestone, but it's simply a product of personal decision making, honoring your word, and pursuing the required action to manifest your definition of success.

Mahatma Gandhi, without a doubt, *became* a larger-than-life figure, someone who *decided* to operate from his true authentic self (True Self), which I define as a state of being where people act authentically and see the world for what it really is based on their expanded paradigms and associated benefits, allowing them to add value to themselves and others at a specific point in time.

Morality and ethics were central to his paradigm formation early on in life as a result of his parents' religious beliefs and his acceptance, exploration, and struggle with the same; however, the largest influence in his life was likely his mother, described as "an extremely pious and religiously devoted lady" (Guna, 2015). She had incredible willpower, which she seems to have passed down to her son along with other strong principles.

Later in life, Gandhi's perspective on religion expanded significantly as he came to understand it from extensive research and discussion with others. He started to practice religion more from a personal level than through the structural systems created by man. This growth mindset allowed him to connect to the true nature of spirituality, which is internal, and allowed him to develop a stronger and deeper sense of morality.

The immortal words of Helen Keller are true of Gandhi's life: "Character cannot be developed in ease and quiet. Only through experience of trial and suffering can the soul be strengthened, ambition inspired, and success achieved." Gandhi's personal experiences changed his lens to the plight of his fellow man, creating in him a desire to improve injustices. It was after he was the victim of severe racism in South Africa that he started organizing. His perspective of "[I'm] a Briton first, and an Indian second" (he was educated in London) was informed when he was spat on, beaten, and segregated from the European whites. He was disturbed and humiliated by these prejudices against him by British people and struggled to comprehend how some people can feel honor, superiority, or pleasure in such inhumane practices (Dhiman, 2016).

Gandhi's life journey and efforts to become self-aware made him unapologetically Gandhi. He developed his true self. While we view Gandhi from a saintly lens, there's a lot of history indicating the truth is more complex. Though there's no doubt he changed the world, his paradigms evolved over time, with him eventually becoming the person we know of today.

Throughout his life journey, he made poor decisions, had many fears—including public speaking (which he faced)—and had numerous biases and prejudices, allowing him to become the historical giant we know of today. He was "just" a human being, like you and me. He lived life based on a set of principles with a strong foundation of morality, ethics, and fairness guiding his paradigm. He made such a big impact because he decided to make a difference in the world, and that journey gave him the courage and self-awareness required for him to succeed.

AUTHENTICITY LEADS TO YOUR TRUE SELF AND GREATER LIFE CONTEXT

Sometimes you hear people say things like "how can one person make any difference?" as an expression of doubt about the impact of a single human in a world of over seven billion people. The ratio of one person to the rest of the global population is less than 0.00000000142. Thus, it's a rational assumption. Then you learn about Mahatma Gandhi, Martin Luther King, Jr. and other "seemingly larger than life" people, and you wonder what would lead to someone being so amazing and powerful as to impact hundreds, thousands, or even millions of people, changing human history in the process. These people seem unreal and not made of the stuff you, me, and other "normal" human beings are made of.

Gandhi and other selfless leaders who have positively impacted the world are regular people who found their true selves after experiencing extensive suffering and struggles leading to self-awareness and authenticity. It was a difficult, incremental process, but one they had to lean into over and over again. They're made of the same stuff we are, and they chose to develop diverse and expanded paradigms. They found the courage to not frequently give in to fear, shame, and other debilitating, personal, limited paradigmatic realities that normally control the rest of us. Just like Neo found out what was wrong with the world, those who have found their true selves see that the out-of-sync personal realities of most humans do not allow them to see the truth—we are fighting ourselves instead of collaborating to fix the needs of humanity—so they set out to fix society's pain points. They have empathy for the rest of us because they themselves were once asleep too, and they understand the powerlessness of the condition. Free from the control of limited paradigms and resulting debilitating negative emotional outputs, they have the power to unleash their talents on the needs of society. They transform themselves into leaders who make a difference to society.

The main difference between *The Matrix* and the real world is that in this reality, the machines are other humans with stuck paradigms, limiting beliefs, and little self-awareness (or massive egos trying to amass power and wealth). Asleep to reality because their world has become narrow, they mainly struggle to deal with their own issues. Fear, shame, guilt, insecurities, and the drama created by stuck paradigms cloud their realities. People with stuck paradigms are slaves to choices decided by fear versus those decided by courage. They are the people we love—our spouses, parents, children, and of course ourselves at many parts of our life journey. The "evil" in the world is not necessarily created by bad people, but by regular folks struggling with issues (relationships, failure, traumas, etc.)—they do not know how or choose not to deal with these struggles. True evil consists of those trying to manipulate these people for their own benefit in search of power and wealth—the result of severely stuck paradigms with runaway egos, people like Hitler and similarly power-hungry politicians and wealthy elites.

People who operate as True Selves see that most humans act powerlessly, so they choose to empower others via their actions. They find purpose in acting on behalf of the greater good. Their expanded paradigms allow them to spend their time not on the jealousy, hate, bitterness, and other negative emotional outputs that are vicious cycles and control our lives and minds, but on efforts making a difference to society. They have strong self-awareness and unusual willpower. They focus on honoring their word and maintaining personal integrity. They are strategic thinkers reflecting on world issues and discussing important matters with others frequently to stay awake. They feel fear but know they must overcome it to keep their personal power and reach higher levels of their true selves. Their goal is to be as authentic as possible and understand the importance of their uniqueness and diverse perspective.

In a world of over seven billion people unaware they are fighting each other for money, power, and control, True Selves see from 30,000 feet. They witness a struggling human race drowning in a glass of water. This is why Greta Thunberg wasn't able to move on from her paradigm after realizing the danger our planet is in; she refused the "blue pill" of blissful naivete, though others did not see the issue as clearly as she did. Because they are their true selves, they choose to help and can operate at a frequency seemingly impossible to those not operating from their authentic selves. They act selflessly.

The dangerous truth is that any of us can operate at this frequency—the purpose of this book is to show you this fact so you can choose the power of authenticity and self-awareness. The only real difference between True Selves and the rest of us is that they fiercely refuse to be anyone other than themselves. They refuse to conform to the false reality so many of us are chasing: realities that keep them enslaved, such as the prioritization of money, power, material things, attention, and other drugs that fire up and feed our inauthenticity.

REDEFINING THE MEANING OF AUTHENTICITY FROM A PARADIGM FRAMEWORK

William H. George (Bill) was my leadership professor at Harvard Business School. His successful career as CEO and Chair of Medtronic, as well as previous jobs before venturing into the academic world, informed his efficacious teaching method. He has written several best-selling leadership books and published articles in major publications. In 2014, the Franklin Institute presented Bill with the Bower Award for Business Leadership. PBS named him one of the "Top 25 Business Leaders of the Past 25 Years."

Based on this impressive biographical description, there's no question he's had a fantastic career which added value to thousands of business professionals, students, and readers globally.

I liked Professor George when I was at HBS. I enjoyed his class and thought him an exceptional professor. Just before the summer of 2005, I asked for his advice regarding an internship I was applying for at Becton Dickinson & Company (BD). He was extremely helpful to me. I sensed his desire to help was genuine, whereas others either were too busy or just helped because they felt like it was their job to do so, which is normal since we were all busy professionals. I had a sense that George provided positive, cheerful help, though I didn't know how to fully process that besides just being grateful to him at the time. Until I started my self-awareness journey, I didn't truly comprehend how valuable his advice, teaching, research, and experiences were to the rest of us.

Bill is also an authority on authentic leadership and his work can be instructional to the rest of us. I finally figured out he was being authentic when he helped me, and I hadn't experienced enough of that in the business world to recognize it as such. Truly authentic business leaders are few and far between, probably smaller in number than the 10 to 15 percent that Dr. Eurich discovered are self-aware, because participants are pursuing for profit measures.

What does it really mean to be authentic? If you act how you feel, does that make you authentic? Can you be born authentic? Is authenticity simply being transparent with your thoughts, emotions, or desires, or is there more to it?

Led by his research, George looks at authenticity from a paradigm framework versus the typical and incomplete way that others view it. There is much discussion on authentic leadership in the business world, but much of it is superficial and describes it from a competent management lens. My issue with their perspective is that I believe someone cannot only be authentic as a business leader. Authenticity is a way of being that has to flow from your paradigm for it to be truly authentic.

As Bill George and his colleagues, Peter Sims, Andrew N. McLean, and Diana Mayer, described in their 2007 *Harvard*

Business Review article, "Discovering Your Authentic Leadership," "discovering your authentic leadership requires a commitment to developing yourself."

The authors describe their research, conducting deep discussions with 125 business leaders. The research was a follow up to Bill George's popular book, *Authentic Leadership*, and set out to answer a key question that CEOs asked when they read the book: "How can people become and remain authentic leaders?" These interviews formed the basis of their article as well as the basis for Bill George's second book, *Discover Your True North*.

George's research and work are foundational because they demonstrate that authentic leaders are not born but created on the basis of a proactive, self-awareness journey as I'm describing in this book, one that's similar to Gandhi's and full of failures, struggles, and incremental actions focused on a desire to improve one's self.

In their article, Bill and his team insist authentic leaders "first and most important [. . .] frame their life stories in ways that allow them to see themselves not as passive observers of their lives but rather as individuals who can develop self-awareness from their experiences. Authentic leaders act on that awareness by practicing their values and principles, sometimes at substantial risk to themselves. They are careful to balance their motivations so that they are driven by these inner values as much as by a desire for external rewards or recognition. Authentic leaders also keep a strong support team around them, ensuring that they live integrated, grounded lives."

Thus, the basis for authentic leadership and authenticity is self-awareness. As we've discussed, it's imperative to expand your paradigm via conversations with people with whom you can be vulnerable to further develop self-awareness.

George and his colleagues also got to understand the factors we discussed in chapter two, which shape paradigms also shape authenticity. "While the life stories of authentic leaders cover the full spectrum of experiences—including the positive impact of parents, athletic coaches, teachers, and mentors—many leaders reported that their motivation came from a difficult experience in their lives. They described the transformative effects of the loss of a job; personal illness; the untimely death of a close friend or relative; and feelings of being excluded, discriminated against, and rejected by peers."

As we discussed, the key is to be resilient and to have a growth mindset. Just like your emotions, we must view difficult experiences as a sensor as well, learning from them instead of letting them negatively impact our paradigms. "Rather than seeing themselves as victims, though, authentic leaders used these formative experiences to give meaning to their lives. They re-framed these events to rise above their challenges and to discover their passion to lead" (George, et al, 2007).

Instead of succumbing to the stuck paradigms of trauma and difficult experiences, the leaders George spoke with (carefully screened and half of which were CEOs) expanded their paradigms and learned from their personal struggles. This is essential to become more self-aware and requires resilience, courage, and a growth mindset. These difficult experiences were important change agents for Gandhi, and from them, he created meaning and purpose in life.

Authenticity requires continuous proactive effort. You must find and work on yourself to operate from your true self. It's impossible to truly be authentic otherwise. As we've discussed throughout this book, we're controlled by System One processes, our emotions, our pasts, and our paradigms. They're severely clouded with a personal reality full of limiting beliefs. There's no way to be authentic in that chaotic mental mess without first focusing on truly understanding ourselves and balancing our paradigms.

Authenticity is an impermanent state of being requiring constant focus, attention, and resilience to emerge.

But the reality is that anyone can be authentic and self-aware. There is no limiting formula, regardless of who you are or your specific circumstances. It does not matter where you are born, how much money you have, or even how educated you are. Some of the most authentic people I have ever met were impoverished neighbors from my village in the Dominican Republic. They had few material possessions but were rich in dignity, integrity, and authenticity, which they valued above anything else. For this reason, sometimes I yearn for the simpler life of country living, where everyone is your family or friend and cares for your well-being, as was the case back home in the late seventies (that may have been my young, innocent paradigm, but the memories are pleasant).

George's research divulged the key formula for authenticity. They asked seventy-five members of the Stanford Graduate

School of Business' Advisory Council to recommend the most important ingredient for leadership development. Almost everyone said self-awareness.

They described the trap I have witnessed so many of my friends experience after college and business school. "Yet many leaders, especially those early in their careers, are trying so hard to establish themselves in the world that they leave little time for self-exploration. They strive to achieve success in tangible ways that are recognized in the external world—money, fame, power, status, or a rising stock price" (George, et al, 2007).

George's research was focused on leaders but applies to everyone. We *all* change and grow during our life and career journeys—our paradigms expand and inform our world view. Our definition of success broadens to include non-pecuniary elements. "As they age, they may find something is missing in their lives and realize they are holding back from being the person they want to be. Knowing their authentic selves requires the courage and honesty to open up and examine their experiences. As they do so, leaders become more humane and willing to be vulnerable" (George, et al, 2007).

I think this explains why I experienced a feeling of betrayal by HBS. Putting aside the fact that an employee was a poor leader, it was the tip of the iceberg for me. I needed double-loop learning to gain self-awareness. I lacked true purpose and meaning in my life, finding them mainly in my HBS volunteering. When that was taken away, I had to take a real good look at myself in the mirror and ask what the meaning of it all was for me. I had embarked on a journey to transform myself and it no longer felt sufficient. Since I had already achieved the socioeconomic transformation I sought, I needed a new journey with a fresh definition of success.

Many people believe authenticity is just being yourself (transparency with your feelings and emotions) or being an authentic leader at work. That would be like saying Vincent van Gogh created an authentic masterpiece the first time he set brush to paper. Quite the contrary. For him to become an original and amazing painter, he had to both find and develop his style. It took decades of focus and active practice. It was a journey of self-discovery full of many trials, tribulations, and real and perceived failures, the most notable being that he never garnered the world's appreciation in his lifetime. It was in fact this lack of acknowledgment or appreciation for his work that led to his demise. However, it was the continuous and incremental effort at improving his craft that led to his becoming a unique and exceptional painter, with numerous masterpieces to boot.

Human authenticity is the manifestation of a masterpiece and requires a similar journey to develop. Any of us can be like Gandhi or the authentic leaders Bill George interviewed, but few of us embark on the journey and do the necessary work. The main reason for this is that we are unaware of how our paradigms function. I had no idea until I was forced to look within myself after my "failure." We do not realize we are not being authentic (we don't know what we don't know)—our personal realities seem to reflect true reality, though as we learned in chapter one, that is not the case. We don't know that we spend most of our lives asleep, operating on autopilot, subconsciously. Thus, self-awareness is required, which itself is an incremental process similar to slowly walking up to the top of a mountain and gradually seeing what is in the other side. You cannot see the other side unless you do the work of climbing up.

None of us can be authentic without first embarking on a journey of self-discovery and understanding ourselves better—how we act, react, what past events weigh heavily on our mind and hold us back, what matters to us, and what our definition of purpose and meaning is. After reading this book, you will be extremely well equipped with the requisite knowledge to successfully embark on this journey.

The truth is I was a reactive, meaning-making machine prior to starting my journey, though I fully believed I was self-aware and authentic. I was not, despite having the right paradigm to achieve my definition of success. I simply did not know what I did not know. I was like a self-driving car programmed to go from one destination to another. I did not fundamentally understand why I wanted to go there, but knew it was an important voyage. However, once I reached the destination, I had to find myself to give meaning to my past efforts and enrich my future decisions in a more purposeful manner. The difficult HBS experience offered me two pills, and I chose the red one.

Self-awareness is a triage process that requires focusing on what's important versus what's fun. It is an incremental process anyone can do.

At some point you will ask yourself, "Why am I here on this planet?" or "What is the purpose of it all?" This is your true self asking you to come home. True authenticity is a hard-fought battle of self-discovery combined with the courage to be vulnerable and to operate from a reality that's closely in sync with the true reality. You cannot do this by being like everyone else. The world is full of problems to solve, but most of us are caught up on the daily dramas wrongly prioritized by our stuck paradigms. That can only change with extensive self-awareness.

You are now ready and fully equipped, so put on your cape and let's get to work!

THE IMPACT OF AUTHENTIC PEOPLE ON MY LIFE

My life has been meaningfully transformed by people operating as True Selves. We all operate from this level when we are not blinded by our stuck paradigms. As an example, when you are selfless, empathetic, loving, understanding, or perform an act of kindness, you are operating from your true authentic self. This is when you significantly impact the lives of other humans.

On the top of the list is my mother, who is probably the most emotionally intelligent and selfless person I've ever met. My mom is the glue that kept us united regardless of how difficult the situation has been for her or any of us. She has no stuck paradigms as far as I can tell (I am sure she does, but my biases blind me). She doesn't hold a grudge, is humble, hates no one, and is selfless. Her morals and ethics are unwavering and she's an inspiration to everyone who knows her.

Grammar School is an extremely important time of life, and I was fortunate to be blessed with some great teachers at Public

School 20 in New York City. My second and third grade teacher, Mrs. Innocencia Cartagena, was also an important person who facilitated our transition when we first moved to the USA. She became a close friend and stayed with us when her husband traveled for business. It was like having a second mother in school during a pivotal time of our youth. She was loving, caring, kind, and went out of her way to make all of us more comfortable in this new land (our whole class consisted of recent immigrants). Furthermore, Barbara Caruso and Judith Horn gave me a love for learning. They inspired me to become academically focused based on their exceptional teaching and motivation skills. My love for learning was born at PS 20 thanks to these transformational teachers.

The most impactful leader in my life is Fr. Jack Podsiadlo, a Jesuit priest who was the principal of Nativity Mission Center. He has been my teacher, mentor, friend, and basically my second father since I met him. He had my family's full support and trust. He taught me that regardless of where I came from, my financial situation, or any other obstacle, I could achieve any goal I set my mind to, with education as the doorway. Fr. Jack provided not only education, but selfless leadership and emotional support/mentorship to students and their immigrant, impoverished families. He's been more important in my personal life than Gandhi and other better-known True Selves can ever be.

Hundreds or perhaps thousands of my fellow students (and their families) see Fr. Jack as a legendary, iconic figure who positively transformed their lives. Thanks to him, I got my first business suit, first job, and attended Xavier High School and Cornell University (he first told me about the school and took me to visit the campus). I'm extremely grateful to the numerous, authentic True Selves who positively impacted my life and my self-awareness.

Who has been a True Self and made a difference in your life? Remember, True Selves are regular people who have flaws just like the rest of us. They also struggle through their journey through life. However, they seize opportunities to add value to the lives of others because they are more self-aware and authentic—a state not constant nor consistent. It is a zig-zagging process just like all other human conditions, but they find a way in those spurts to add value to others and to society. When you think about the True Selves in your life, don't search for larger-than-life figures, but everyday people who positively impacted your life and helped you become the parts of yourself that you are most proud of.

HOW TO FIND YOUR AUTHENTIC SELF

One characteristic every human has in common is that we are born completely unique. There's no one like you on the entire planet today or in its vast history. You'll only exist for your lifetime—no one will ever be or think exactly like you. The universe has a one-shot chance at you, so you're nothing short of a miracle. You live once and there are no do-overs.

Your life, though impacted by where you were born, who your parents are, relationships, and other characteristics I discussed in chapter two, will be largely your choice. Yes, you'll have numerous obstacles and it will not be easy, but that will be the case for everyone else. That's the human condition. But then, why are so many people trying so hard to be like others? Why do we refuse to pursue our true authentic selves? What's the appeal of inauthenticity since most of us live this way? Why must society experience mass powerlessness as a result of our attraction to synthetic selves?

As we established in past chapters, the answer is fear, shame, and insecurity. We want to be liked and connected to others and we don't believe we're worthy or good enough, so we fail to be vulnerable and share our real selves, creating limiting beliefs and stuck paradigms that are an enslaving, vicious cycle. We get stuck living a life of powerlessness, on autopilot and numb to reality. The power of your words and those of others' means that judgments, complaining, and the harsh rhetoric leading to fear, shame, and insecurity also lead to us becoming inauthentic versions of ourselves. We give up our power. Our limited paradigms cause us to give up and we inadvertently choose blissful naivete over the effort required to see ourselves and life for what it truly is.

One significant and modern hurdle making our journey of self-discovery more difficult today is our participation in the world of internet content and social media. With apps like Facebook, Tik Tok, and numerous others, we can confirm our incomplete self-perceptions and make them seem rational or even superior to the views of others. We form communities of likeminded people who support specific points of views even if they are wrong or have evil biases or negative emotional outputs.

We feel empowered to belong to such groups and become convinced our perspectives are both correct and rational. Even more dangerous, these apps depend on feeding us information we are passionate about based on our clicks, which will further embed our paradigms in specific, even if incorrect, ways of seeing the world by giving us the illusion of knowledge. As the great astrophysicist Stephen Hawking once said, "The greatest enemy of knowledge is not ignorance, it is the illusion of knowledge."

Unless we reach a level of self-awareness, we will remain numb, inauthentic versions of ourselves trying to copy other people instead of finding and celebrating our uniqueness. Martin Luther King, Jr., Albert Einstein, Gandhi, Wolfgang Amadeus Mozart, Leonardo da Vinci, Nelson Mandela, Mother Teresa, Greta Thunberg, and others are described as larger than life because they were authentic and took the road less traveled, but they were struggling human beings just like you and me. They are special because they added purpose and meaning to their lives by making a difference to others and society. There are many more people who fit this description, though they are not well known. You know many of them yourself.

I believe my mother and several of my teachers and mentors fit this category extremely well. They gave me access to personal power and freed me from the debilitating chains of stuck paradigms. And you, if you chose to be your true self, can be one. Which people in your life fit this description?

According to Caroline McHugh—keynote speaker, teacher, coach, and author of *Never Not a Lovely Moon*—in her TED Talk, *The Art of being Yourself*, the only time you attempt to be you is when something catastrophic happens forcing you to be vulnerable, such as the death of a loved one or something that rocks the core of your being. She believes it's then you ask yourself this key question and truly ponder it: "Who do you think you are?"

Caroline thinks you should ask yourself the same question when you're in a position of strength instead, so you can find your true self. I agree. The question is intended to have you search deep into your paradigm and find your authenticity. As I personally discovered, we don't seek authenticity until we lose meaning and purpose in life.

We should be asking ourselves this question in grammar school, middle school, high school, college, and basically every year of our existence. Our parents and our teachers should help us think about this key question occasionally so we have a better sense of self as adults. Furthermore, I think we must ask the question of ourselves often and answer it from a principled perspective, a place of courage, so we can define and redefine who we are. Awareness and self-improvement should be considered just as important as academic knowledge. Though we don't know it, we are strangers to ourselves for most of our lives and don't realize we operate from a place of inauthenticity most of the time. We leave so much power on the table.

Caroline also believes that "when you find out how to be yourself, it is an incredibly liberating and un-tragic way to go through life, so you don't develop an identity that is predicated on being patchwork personality. You are not a composite or amalgam of your experiences and influences. You are not just somebody's boss, of somebody's mom or anybody's anything. You are yourself" (McHugh, 2013). Based on her research and experience, Caroline believes we all have four versions of ourselves which create the complex patchwork personality of humans:

1. **The Perceived You:** This is what everybody else thinks of you. It's the you that you showcase to the outside world, to society—your gender, the color of your skin, height, what you wear, and various other factors. Because there are billions of people in the world, their opinion of you will be mixed—we all see life from our individual paradigms. However, understanding how the world may see you from a contextual point of view is important for your self-awareness. Caroline believes it's debilitating to need other people's approval to be yourself. She says "you will never be perception-less but it's important to be perception free." From our paradigm framework, we know to be someone requiring the approval of others to be happy is the result of limiting believes and stuck paradigms. Thus, to be perception-free requires paradigm expansion to get proper context and see reality (McHugh, 2013).

2. **Your Persona:** This is your "wish image." It's the image you'd like everybody else to have of you. This you will continue to move and change based on your experiences, conversations, and self-dialogue/reflections. I believe this is the you most susceptible to fear, and, as I described in chapter three, is where your desire to connect leads to a lack of vulnerability. As a result, your persona is the most significant source of your inauthenticity (McHugh, 2013).

3. **Your Ego:** Your ego is what you think of you. The problem with this version of you, according to McHugh, "is that

some days you feel invincible and other days you feel inadequate." Caroline says "those are two extremes of your ego and one of them is about self-congratulations and the other is about self-castigation." She believes your entire life has been about building a stable relationship with your ego. You need an ego to survive in this world, but the key is to move it from its dominant position to one of service, which comes from equilibrium. Caroline believes this comes from inside of you and creates confidence. She asserts that "you have to develop an inner state of mind that is impervious to" the good stuff and bad stuff that will happen to you. I agree and believe the state of mind she is describing is achieved via expanded paradigms, which will provide context and subsequent equilibrium to your ego, as you'll be seeing reality from unclouded lenses (McHugh, 2013).

4. **Self:** The self is "the you that you are when you were born, that you will be when you die." It's the ever present, unchanging you—your true self. Caroline describes this as sort of a mystic you, but I believe this is you when you see the world from expanded paradigms and connect to reality in a way that allows you to see others clearly and see their humanity and struggles. From that perspective, this you is selfless and acts in the service of humanity. This you balances a runaway ego through which a person acts in complete service of themselves. It's the you that gets lost by the creation of stuck paradigms and limiting beliefs but can be freed with self-awareness and a properly cultivated paradigm (McHugh, 2013).

We should choose who we are from a place of authenticity and proactively do all we can to operate from that self, using all the tools at our disposal, including but not limited to the Emotional Output Process, Double-Loop Learning, The Iceberg Model on Emotion, and other tools speaking to us. This will allow us to be true to ourselves.

Being your true self is a journey that will no doubt require hard work and sacrifice and cause pain, but it will give purpose and meaning to yourself, your family and friends, and the rest of society. You have to expose your inauthenticity so you can know when you are being that person. We don't all have to be like Gandhi or Martin Luther King, Jr. Imagine a world where artists, engineers, teachers, bartenders, and everyone else operated from their true authentic selves. What would society look like? We all should be authentic to give meaning to our lives.

SO WHAT DOES THIS MEAN FOR YOUR PARADIGM?

As the title of this chapter suggests, you can only access reality when you are your true self. Allowing ourselves to be controlled by fear and stuck paradigms means we live in a separate reality from the rest of society, one that only exists in our minds—one that takes away our power.

Furthermore, when we operate from a place of authenticity, we better understand our purpose in life as we can clearly see the needs and struggles of our fellow human beings. We are also able to help, freed from being weighed down by the limiting beliefs and other internal obstacles that normally create a focus on the self, a runaway ego, and the inability to operate authentically.

Principle 9: Self-awareness will lead to authenticity, which allows you to make a difference to others and to society. It is a life-long journey that, though few opt in to, anyone can traverse. This temporary state of being requires continuous work and effort to maintain or uncover.

CHAPTER 10

Cultivating a Principle-Centered Paradigm

——

*"People will do anything, no matter how
absurd, to avoid facing their own soul."*

—CARL JUNG

Humans and society need mirrors—the ability to see and face
the obvious, difficult truths, versus the convenient truths we
tell ourselves—to be able to expand our paradigms, improve
ourselves, and positively impact reality. Mirrors are a way to
increase our authenticity, revealing the truth as distinct from
our personal reality, which is obscured by stuck paradigms.
The truth offers us a principle-centered paradigm with access
to morality and our true selves.

Modern advances in psychological theory demonstrate that
our actions can be both subconscious and immoral due to
System One and other systemic processes. We all operate in

this manner. Can some of the biases and prejudices we inflict on ourselves, such as racism, be stuck paradigms and/or subconscious System One processes we birth into the world as a collection of paradigms which create our society? If so, how can they be unstuck?

The 2007 American biographical drama film *The Great Debaters,* directed by and starring Denzel Washington, is a mirror of America and its citizens witnessing the injustices of a segregated Jim Crow south during the Great Depression in the 1930s. It depicts the internal and external struggles of African Americans as well as the nation as a whole. As with all hard truths, it's a difficult movie to watch, and yet it offers a true picture of our society at a transformational time.

Strong evidence for the inconvenience and hard truth delivered by this exceptional movie is demonstrated by its poor performance at the box office. Despite the fact the movie was released via Harpo Productions (Oprah Winfrey), hit theaters during Christmas (one of the most popular times for box office hits), features a superb cast (Denzel Washington and Forest Whitaker are both Academy Award winners), and was nominated for several awards including Best Picture, its total earnings of thirty million dollars was simply pathetic (IMDB, 2007). It offered such hard truths that we refused to face it even as a movie. What are we so afraid of?

Let's try to understand what makes this movie such an unpleasant mirror and memory of how we have treated other human beings.

Wiley College, a historically black college in Texas, is home to a promising debate team that, after an undefeated season, will debate Harvard and draw the attention of the entire nation at a time when race tensions are high.

Wiley's debate coach, Professor Melvin B. Tolson, is portrayed as a radical. Outside of school he's empowering African Americans to unionize (at a risk to his life). In school, he's showing students how to use their voices to create a national discussion about the pros and cons of racism. Tolson is aware of his label and tells a parent who confronts him regarding the dangers that "Jesus was also radical."

He informs those that tried out for the team that "out of 360 students here at Wiley College, only forty-five of you are brave enough to try out for the debate team. Of that forty-five, only four of you will remain standing. Why? Because Debate is blood-sport, it's combat. But your weapons are words." He tells them "there is a revolution going on in the north [. . .]. They are changing the way negros think. I am talking about poets like Hughes, Bennett, Zora Neale Hurston, Countee Cullen."

This scene is poignant because a silent revolution is also going on in our world in relation to self-awareness. Thanks to Daniel Kahneman, Brené Brown, and numerous other leaders, we're discovering that our perceived reality is not as we think we understand it. That much effort and focus is required for us to operate in true reality and free ourselves from the personal mental bondage we created throughout our lives. Those not pursuing this type of self-improvement are being manipulated, as Jim Baggot warned, either by those who understand the process, or by the "blue pill" of self-denial with which we self-medicate.

The most powerful scene in the movie occurs when the debaters and Tolson come upon an angry mob that has just lynched an African American man. Having just committed this despicable injustice, a mob leader says, "There are niggers in that car," and the crowd chases them with an intent to kill them as well because of the color of their skin. Though they get away, you can imagine the mental trauma, resulting paradigm crisis, and fear that follows such an experience for the debaters.

Can you see any parallels today to folks who are brain-washed and fed misinformation? The modern way we're being divided may not only include our skin color but our beliefs. Are there groups today you notice acting violently because they were fed misinformation about politics, voting, the existence of COVID-19, and the effectiveness of a vaccine to combat the disease?

At Harvard, the debaters must argue on the importance of members of society following the rule of law. In the last round, a Harvard debater delivers a fantastic argument about following the rule of law. The rebuttal, broadcasting live via radio to the entire nation, is delivered by a brilliant, nervous, and self-aware fourteen-year-old based on his personal experience:

"In Texas, they lynch negros. My teammates and I saw a man strangled by his neck and set on fire. We drove through a lynch mob, pressed our faces against the floorboard. I looked at my teammates. I saw the fear in their eyes, and worse, the shame. What was this negro's crime that he should be hung without trial in a dark forest filled with a mob? Was he a thief? Was he a killer? Or just a negro? Was he a sharecropper? A preacher? Were his children waiting up for him?"

He described their experience, and the vivid, verbal picture offers listeners a vulnerable mirror into their traumatic experience. His perspective humanizes African Americans for those with an uninformed opinion on race matters and its impacts. He illustrates how their hatred, opinions, judgments, and/or inaction have societal consequences on innocent human beings. He concludes by forcing them to search their souls regarding the morality of the situation, and issues a threat understood as a personal responsibility of any oppressed group.

"And who are we to just lie there and do nothing? No matter what he did, the mob was the criminal. But the law did nothing, just left us wondering. Our opponent says nothing that erodes the rule of law can be moral, but there is no rule of law in the Jim Crow South. Not when negroes are denied housing, turned away from schools, hospitals, and not when we are lynched. St Augustine said an unjust law is no law at all. Which means I have a right, even a duty to resist, with violence or civil disobedience. You should pray I choose the latter."

To suggest I can even start to comprehend what African Americans felt during this pivotal historical period would be an inauthentic limiting belief on my part. I can try to imagine, but I could not fully understand. I can, however, acknowledge it was horrible, and as a human and an American, I'm ashamed this is our history.

I can also understand the film is too painfully true for many of us to watch and relive mentally. Carl Jung was correct when he said that "people will do anything, no matter how absurd, to avoid facing their own soul." However, mustering up the courage to do so will lead to a significantly better, more expanded paradigm, and a view to the true reality. We must look in the mirror often so we can understand ourselves and not repeat the mistakes of the past. That goes for each of us individually and for society as a whole.

We may be too afraid to face our darkness and our true selves.

But we *must*.

DEVELOPING A PRINCIPLE-CENTERED PARADIGM

A principle-centered paradigm—living life by a predetermined set of moral and ethical tenets—is critical for being your authentic true self and can only be reached by frequently looking in the mirror of our darkness. Morality and ethics are learned behaviors we get from the external world; however, right and wrong are not always clearly defined. We've recently concluded that the traditional psychological model of ethics, which originated from Aristotle and other great philosophers, is flawed.

It assumes people are rational and will adequately weigh right and wrong to make informed decisions on moral issues. From that perspective, American society should never have developed with the racism and injustice portrayed in *The Great Debaters*. The signs are everywhere that individuals don't make decisions based on traditional psychological theory in most situations. We are controlled by our paradigms.

We would not have allowed ourselves to be at the heights of ethical injustices after balanced moral consideration. While some may have acted selfishly in creating such a reality, the majority would have accurately weighed the detrimental societal consequences of repressing people merely on the basis of their skin color, especially as a Judeo-Christian nation. But there's no question American history is this ugly. That is the simple truth.

There's something else at play here which would explain how irrational moral human behavior leads to society's unjust laws and our own clouded moral judgment.

A paradigm shift has occurred recently which now places Behavioral Ethics as a superior way of evaluating moral behavior than traditional moral theory. According to *Ethics Unwrapped*, a program by the McCombs School of Business, "traditional philosophical approaches focus on defining moral theory and understanding the very concepts of right and wrong. Behavioral ethics, on the other hand, examines how we make moral decisions and offers insights into how we can be our best selves."

They describe Behavioral Ethics as a fairly new science that utilizes learning from behavioral psychology, cognitive science, neuroscience, evolutionary biology, and other fields. "Its findings show that people are often influenced, subconsciously, by psychological biases, organizational and social pressures, and situation factors that impact decision making and can lead to unethical action."

As we learned in chapter one from the excellent work of Daniel Kahneman, humans are irrational. This fact has a substantial impact on our ethical behavior. What this means is that to truly develop a principle-centered paradigm, self-awareness is required just like it is for authenticity. System One Processes and Heuristic shortcuts also lead us astray morally.

Essentially, we fool ourselves into dishonest behavior with one side of our brains by hiding it from the other side so we can be okay with our conscience. Our mind will eventually become aware of the situation and by that time, it may be too late. We trap ourselves to suffer the consequences of unethical behavior.

According to an article by Cara Biasucci and Robert Prentice, titled "Teaching Behavioral Ethics (Using 'Ethics Unwrapped' Videos and Educational Materials)," what this means is that "good people do bad things because of the influence of social and organizational pressures, cognitive heuristics and biases, and a variety of situational factors." This resource attempts to demonstrate that business schools need better ethics education. I couldn't agree more. We *all* need to understand how our internal systems evaluate and make ethical decisions, especially if we can be immoral unconsciously.

To demonstrate that there is evidence of unintentional immorality, the authors point to the book *Why They Do It: Inside the Mind of the White-Collar Criminal* by Harvard Law School professor Eugene Soltes. As part of his research for his book, Soltes befriended some of the highest profile white-collar criminals, including Bernie Madoff, Andy Fastow, Dennis Kozlowski, and numerous other infamous former business "leaders." He arrived at the astonishing conclusion that "they were not so different from the rest of us." Biasucci and Prentice shared Soltes' conclusion that "in our own small ways, we are all susceptible to making the same mistakes as these former executives."

So how can we make better moral decisions, knowing our susceptibility to System One and other mental processes which lead us morally astray? The article offers this suggestion from Eugene Soltes' book: "Appreciating our lack of invincibility—our inherent weakness and frailty—offers us the best chance of designing the appropriate mechanisms to help manage these limitations."

We must a question our gut feelings in new or difficult situations because they can be heuristic shortcuts from our System One processes. In other words, we have to be self-aware and not allow ourselves to be on autopilot, which may not always be possible. Since we do not always make decisions consciously, having other people who question us would also be helpful.

As the author warns, we have to be vulnerable and honest with ourselves. "If we humbly recognize that we might not always even notice the choices that will lead us astray, we are more likely to develop ways to identify and control those decisions. But it's only when we realize that our ability to err is much greater than we often think it is that we'll begin to take the necessary steps to change and improve" (Soltes, 2016).

It seems to me the best solution is adhering to Clayton Christensen's rule of never giving in to Marginal Thinking. In the case of morality, as in the case with honoring your word, "100 percent is easier than 98 percent" if we are to maintain a principle-centered paradigm. Marginal Thinking is a slippery slope, and our mental shortcuts will repeat our moral behavior continuously.

But even that may not be enough. Our automatic mental processes causes us to be unethical at times, so we must be honest with ourselves about how we function to limit the potential damage. The only real way to create a principle-centered paradigm is to realize we're flawed, imperfect beings. We must understand how we function by becoming more self-aware. We cannot leave our morality to System One processes, which is what typically happens.

REPERCUSSIONS OF MY UNETHICAL CONDUCT

When I was in the fifth grade, my schoolmate Hector started to bother me during lunch time in the P.S. 20 playground. He was trying to show off to his friends. He kept challenging me to a fight—one I was trying to avoid. Unbeknownst to him, I had a lot of experience in physical fights by that time, but I was skinny, and he underestimated the risk I posed.

I was involved in numerous fights from age eight to twelve. Altercations may have been how I dealt with the many changes I experienced in my youth. My parents moved to the USA when I was about seven, leaving us with my grandmother. At nine, I was brought to this new country and to a massive city vastly different than my village. Back home I knew everyone, but here we were all strangers. Everything was different, including the language, the food, the people, and the concrete jungle. I had no friends and missed the freedom of the Dominican countryside.

Our school was comprised of numerous immigrant boys. We all felt like outsiders. Hector hung out with a group of friends who had all been born here—the sons of immigrants. They knew the ropes and felt at home. This was their turf. His little group would make fun of us recent immigrants because we didn't speak English well or dressed "funny." I was a quiet kid, so I probably seemed like an easy target.

I wasn't a bad kid, but the substantially larger world I entered offered major changes I could not comprehend. Fighting was perhaps my way of grasping for some sense of control. I delighted in my wins and did not see a problem with the violence. It seemed like the natural order of things from my perspective.

As I got more acclimated to my new environment, conflicts decreased and I transitioned to less brutal means of control, such as focusing on academics, spending time with new friends, and trying out new sports like dodgeball and basketball. I was no longer eager to control my external environmental with a display of brute force because it would impact my relationships and ability to participate in these sports.

However, when Hector started to taunt me again that afternoon, I'd had enough. I was ready to teach him a lesson. Surrounded by dozens of kids who delighted in being spectators to such childish violence, Hector quickly learned he was no match for me. *The odd-looking skinny kid with mismatching clothes can fight*, he must have thought. Based on his pathetic attempt at the art, I wondered if it was his first time trying to be a tough guy. By the time the teacher pulled us apart, his face had suffered several injuries while I barely broke a sweat. I specifically recall a girl on whom I had a crush triumphantly lifting my arms and declaring me the winner. It was a surreal feeling, but not in a positive, victorious kind of way.

"Victorious" was the last descriptor I would have used to judge myself after the bout. It felt like a very different experience than previous fights. First, we were caught and sent to the principal's office; it was my first time there, so I was scared and ashamed. Second, I had inflicted some very serious-looking injuries on Hector's face. Sitting across from him in the principal's office, I felt absolutely horrendous about what I had done to another human being. I just stared at him in disbelief. He was crying with pain, but I wept with horror at the feeling of the immorality of my actions. I was a monster, and the realization hit the core of my conscience. I felt incredulous at my ability to inflict injuries on another person, even if he was a bully.

It was a pivotal experience for me and shifted my paradigm to one of nonviolence. It was my last fight, and by far my most memorable.

I faced a part of me full of darkness that day; a part I had never acknowledged. After previous fights, I would be surrounded by eager boys who supported or judged the bout, not on its ethics, but on whether I had won or lost. Winning was everything on the playground. It was an ego trip, and my mind justified my actions. The repercussions to the other person (physical or mental) were not much of a concern, nor something to which I gave any thought previously. I was usually on the winning side, celebrating victories. When I lost, I was plotting how to win and thinking about more violence. This time, I felt like I experienced the repercussion of my actions as an outsider, so I was able to really see the truth. It was like a mirror.

Winning on the playground seemed harmless, though I am sure paradigms were shaped based on those events. Mine sure was. However, those same boys grow up and work on Wall Street or some other playground where it's still all about winning. The ethical nature of the wins, especially the small ones, isn't given much thought, thereby solidifying the processes by which we gain money and power. That is why those and other jobs tend to be filled with males—we're basically modern hunters, in a sense. Work becomes just another playground where we fight and assuage our egos. After all, everyone does it, so it's just survival— or we justify our actions by telling ourselves that, at least.

This is exactly the type of thinking behavioral ethics researchers warn led to the downfall of people like Jeffrey Skilling. Little by little, you commit unethical acts that don't seem to mean much. Like a staircase, these acts become bigger and bigger. And then you get caught.

The point that I'm trying to make here is that I never stopped to really think about what I was doing. I knew that I'd get in trouble if I fought. Thus, from a traditional philosophical perspective, I knew it was "wrong." I understood that fighting wasn't socially acceptable behavior, but I never fully contemplated the act and categorized it as unethical or "not who I was." It lived in another part of my brain, far from my conscience, until I was held accountable for my decisions and forced to truly reflect on them with Hector's battered face sitting across from me.

If I had to guess, I'd say my fighting persona was best friends with my ego. I think that's how humans truly operate. We convince ourselves that, as long as we don't get caught, pretty much anything is okay if it gives us pleasure, power, or another benefit. We find ways to compartmentalize wrong behavior, reaping its benefits, and don't define it as unethical, especially if we can point to others doing it. For some reason, if it's socially acceptable, we believe it's okay—but that isn't true, since we are not rational beings.

It's actually worse than that. We believe things like, "If I do it, it is not unethical because I am not a bad person." That slippery slope of a thought leads to incredible unethical heights.

And we all feel that way at times!

Does this remind you of "defensive reasoning" in double-loop learning? It should, because that feeling is the tip of the iceberg and will lead to serious problems if not addressed, as the white-collar criminals in Soltes' book found out. Since our paradigms are systems, the key is to be aware that we operate in this manner. We must hold ourselves accountable, not only for our behavior, but for the "why" of our actions. We have to revisit the double-loop learning system and understand our unethical behavior is a result of a certain aim or goal we're pursuing (first single-loop thinking)—such as money or power. However, we may still be acting like we're on the middle school playground trying to control our foreign environment.

Just like Gandhi is merely a man with expanded paradigms and access to reality, Jeffrey Skilling and the rest are just men with clouded paradigms and murky realities. We can be either of them—the only difference is our paradigms.

FACING OUR DARKNESS TO INCREASE SELF-AWARENESS

Will Sparks, PhD, the Dennis Thompson Chair and Professor of Leadership at the McColl School of Business at Queens University of Charlotte, believes that "self-awareness is foundational for reaching our highest potential. Unfortunately, I believe that our culture has narrowly defined self-awareness today to talk about it only in terms of your strengths [. . .]. That is an important part of the self-awareness equation but showing your strengths is only half. If you are going to celebrate your light, you are also going to have to understand your darkness."

In his excellent TED Talk, *The Power of Self-Awareness*, Sparks describes his experience while attending a doctoral program at George Washington University, where he was forced to face his darkness. In one of his classes, he had

Professor Jerry B. Harvey, PhD, who helped him acknowledge difficult truths and meaningfully improved his life as a result. Based on that difficult growth experience, Sparks developed a three-step process he believes is imperative for reaching self-awareness.

First, he's convinced true "self-awareness does not comfort, it disturbs and disrupts." It hurts and it is scary, but if you want to truly improve yourself, you have to be willing to face your darkness. "It is in that disruption that we are afforded an opportunity for true growth and development" (Sparks, 2021).

Sparks' use of the word "darkness" describes my stuck paradigm framework. The darkness is a negative experience or discussion that resulted in limiting beliefs and a stuck paradigm. You can only access reality by facing and expanding your paradigm, which Sparks described as reaching self-awareness. I fully agree. The only way to reach self-awareness is to fully explore and understand your paradigms. The consequences of my fight with Hector led to me facing my darkness and the immorality of violence. It fundamentally changed how I related to it forever. I now firmly believe in nonviolence, but only as a result of the self-awareness from that experience.

In the immortal words of Robert Frost, "The best way out is always through" (Filkins, 2020).

His second piece of insight is that "we have a moral obligation to give constructive, developmental feedback to those in our lives" (Sparks, 2021). He says we're all guilty of sugarcoating the truth because we are afraid to say what we really feel. As a result, we censor ourselves because we believe the truth may disturb and anger our loved ones. However, in so doing we're robbing them of the opportunity to achieve self-awareness by facing their darkness. They may not be happy about it, but it will be helpful for them to see and hear the truth.

I fully agree with Sparks that we have this moral obligation. It will help our loved ones and our fellow man. However, based on my experience doing this, we must first be vulnerable and truly listen to what they have to say to inspire vulnerability in them as well. I believe it's difficult for people with stuck paradigms to see reality based on their hazy paradigms. The discussion needs to be set up properly to maximize effectiveness—otherwise, it may not work. I've failed in this area repeatedly, only to understand the person's stuck paradigms and their inability or unwillingness to admit or see that prevented them from benefiting from what I believed was the truth. Despite this obstacle, Sparks is right and effort must be taken to get to the truth.

Finally, Sparks believes that "personal transformation can only occur when we have the courage to face our own shadow." In addition to the sadness, guilt, or other difficult feelings from facing your darkness, you'll have an incredible sense of liberation. Thus, seeing both your strengths and your darkness is the best way to know yourself.

Basically, what Sparks is saying is that we must have the courage to face our paradigms in order to personally transform ourselves. Furthermore, he believes that instead of comforting people and inauthentically telling them what they want to hear, we have to be honest and tell hard truths leading to paradigm expansion. This is a self-aware perspective most people will not agree with, but I'm wholeheartedly on his side. He is right.

In addition to the mirror the students showed the nation in *The Great Debaters*, which led to improving race relations, this also applies to ourselves. We must be honest with ourselves and admit we continuously struggle with ethical and moral behavior. It is not simply a matter of creating a specific set of principles to live by. Yes, that's essential. However, the way to authenticity is to realize that just like with self-awareness, it's a journey and we will continually struggle to be morally and ethically correct.

We'll make mistakes and will at times consciously choose the wrong path. We must forgive ourselves and restart the process, understanding it's a human condition and we need to strengthen our ethical muscles to access our true authentic selves.

SO WHAT DOES THIS MEAN FOR YOUR PARADIGM?

Throughout our lives, we will continuously have the opportunity to face hard truths. Many will be about ourselves or the people we love. We have a choice. We can either accept and face the truth and do something about it, or allow fear, shame, and guilt to create stuck paradigms. To access reality, we must honestly face our issues and deal with truth proactively.

There is a part of *The Great Debaters* movie that mentions Antaeus, the gigantic wrestler in Greek mythology. Defeat would make him stronger. When he was thrown down to the earth, he would get up and become more powerful.

This is a good way to look at our ethical behavior as it relates to our paradigms. We will commit immoral and unethical actions throughout our lives—we are only human. We will make choices knowing that we're being unethical, or we will find ourselves in immoral situations unintentionally as described above. We must acknowledge and face both and realize that we were being inauthentic. If we're honest with ourselves, we will learn, expand our paradigms and, like Antaeus, become stronger. However, if we don't acknowledge that we erred, the resulting liming beliefs and stuck paradigms will be our undoing and result in a life of inauthenticity and a state of powerlessness.

But the reality is that this is a purposeful and incremental life-long journey through which we will constantly struggle. This shall be the case for every single one of us and was the case for all of history's larger-than-life figures. The process reminds me of the Bible's stance on sin. We are all sinners, and we will continue to be sinners. Our sins are large in number and, just like the discussion on inauthenticity, can be overwhelming with all the requirements to overcome its grips. It is a lot to process since we have limited cognitive capacity. We need to acknowledge the barriers to a good paradigm, but we may need to pursue changes in them incrementally.

As an example, during Yom Kippur, every person praying in the synagogue acknowledges the sins they have committed as a group. Catholic confession is similar in that we stand in front of a priest and reveal numerous sins that have been committed and resolve to stop repeating them. My sense is that the only real change comes when we decide to pick one of those sins and start fixing it, committing to move on to others as the first ones are overcome.

For our society to advance and not get stuck with the chosen injustices of those in power, courageous men and women must also provide constructive, developmental feedback to those in our lives, as advised by William Sparks. We have to face our individual and societal darkness to access the truth. We have to accept that self-awareness will disrupt us but also free us to be more powerful.

Principle 10: We must have the courage to face our true mirrors and our light as well as our darkness full of difficult truths, to become optimally self-aware and develop a principle-centered paradigm.

CHAPTER 11

Make Relationships Your Top Priority

"You don't develop courage by being happy in your relationships every day. You develop it by surviving difficult times and challenging adversity."

—EPICURUS

As Elie Weisel, the famous author and Holocaust survivor said, "Just as despair can come to one only from other human beings, hope, too, can be given to one only by other human beings." Relationships are the most powerful force guiding your paradigms. Though at times you take them for granted, they are the engine of your purpose and meaning, or lack thereof.

Simply said, relationships are the single most important priority of your life. If you don't understand and acknowledge that, the hard truth is that your paradigms are blurred, and you are missing the whole point of existence. This difficult truth of minimizing the importance of relationships applies to us all throughout our lives, unfortunately. It takes away our power.

Relationships should be recognized as your largest source of power. The only reason to have power is to receive and bestow specific benefits to other humans and to yourself. However, we allow the drama and traumas from our paradigms to disconnect us from this realization. We use our careers and numerous other excuses to minimize the importance of those whom we love, especially when we feel it can hurt us emotionally.

Relationships are also the single biggest source of and reason for our constant meaning making.

Think about every movie you've ever seen or book you've read. The majority, if not all, deal with the emotional outputs of relationships, such as love, jealousy, hate, hope, etc., in one way, shape, or form. All of Shakespeare's plays or poems, for example, are about relationships. Some end in tragedies, others in marriage, but all are about the feelings created by lovers, adversaries, family members, and the resulting happiness or chaos that ensues.

A good movie example is the 2005 film *Castaway*, starring Tom Hanks. Though the majority of the film is about how a castaway survives after a plane crash that leaves him isolated on a remote island, his purpose for survival becomes the desire to be reunited with his girlfriend, for whom he was too busy before his misfortune. He's so lonely that he utilizes a volleyball to create a human companion, Wilson. His discussions with Wilson preserve his sanity and motivate him to survive. When he loses the volleyball, on which he painted a human face, he experiences deep sadness, as if a close human friend had truly died, because in his paradigm, it really did. Upon returning to civilization, he finally understands the importance of relationships and will no longer take them for granted. This is a powerful representation about how our paradigms function.

Relationships impact our view of reality in fundamental ways. Based on the strong box office sales for *Castaway* at $430 million, it's evident we can all relate to Tom Hanks' character in some way (Pirnia, 2016).

GETTING PLUGGED IN

Humans are born truly unique and independent of each other, as Caroline McHugh mentioned in her TED Talk, *The Art of Being Yourself.* This is evident by watching how kids act before age seven. They are fearless. Their paradigms have no limits and they have a natural growth mindset. Children are vulnerable, authentic, and speak their minds without concerns for the feelings of others. This is probably why Jesus encourages us to be more like children. They are authentic.

However, at some point, based on their perception of how society functions (or perhaps how parents protect/treat them), kids begin to act like they're actually interdependent on human relationships. My daughter was absolutely fearless until age six or seven. She would sing, act, and showcase her talents to anyone at any time, but became more reserved around seven years of age. For some reason, at this general age, kids experience fear or other emotions that limit their freedoms of expression and their actions as they relate to other people. They begin to care about what others will "think" of them and create limits to what they say, do, and/or express, as well as how they dress/look.

This is the beginning of a lifetime of creating emotional outputs because of other people, and the purposeful limitation of their vulnerability due to fears of being judged. We give away massive amounts of power when our actions are dependent on other people. However, we all fear the judgments of parents, friends, and even strangers.

We should view this not as an end, but as the beginning of our self-awareness journey. Relationships allow us to see life from unique and different perspectives outside of our paradigms. The challenge is if we don't remain (or find/create) our authentic selves in the process, we may get lost in this journey, never to resurface again.

In a sense, the beginning of this social dependence is like a light going out on our uniqueness. Paradigms become stuck or limited based on our interactions and dependence on other humans. They also expand in other ways as we share our paradigms with others. We get exposed to new ways of thinking and being.

I suspect it's this feeling of interdependence leading to many of the issues of relationships. Instead of celebrating our uniqueness, we try to control each other and use our talents for self-gain instead of kindness. It's this difference in how we act that makes self-awareness so important. If you project these variations onto the rest of society, it is the difference between war and peace, ignorance or advancement, and apocalypse or evolution. Our ability to control our emotions, to be self-aware, and to cultivate our paradigms has evolutionary implications.

It is therefore the beginning of a new life journey where we should loudly ask the question, "Who am I?" The answer should be a resounding, "I am myself." With self-awareness and paradigm cultivation, we can see others for who they truly are and use our relationships to positively shape and guide who we are and want to become in our own life journey, instead of trying to become like other people.

Whether we like it or not, the only way to get through life is via relationships that will challenge us in ways which reveal who we really are.

SOCIAL SCIENCE LINKS OUR BIOLOGICAL PROCESSES TO OUR RELATIONSHIPS

Daniel Goleman's latest book, *Social Intelligence: The New Science of Human Relationships*, is based on social neuroscience, a subject matter that can help us understand how relationships impact us. According to Goleman, social neuroscience tells us that "our brains are mainly designed to connect to the brains of other people" (*Expanded Books*, 2006). This new science seeks to understand what's going on and what happens inside our brains when we interact with other humans.

The goal of social neuroscience is to understand the psychological processes underlying our social behavior (Ito and Kubota, 2021).

The findings of this new branch of science are surprising. A simple illustrative example that Goleman cites is when a woman stares directly into the eyes of a man, it triggers the release of dopamine, a neurotransmitter of pleasure (*Expanded Books*, 2006). This and numerous other examples demonstrate that the social brain is an invisible connector for the biological function of our species. Thus, there's a direct connection/interaction between social connections and relationships that can be measured inside our brains. Scientists use numerous types of methods to observe mental impact of social behavior, such as brain imaging, and can prove other people can enact biological changes in your body. Effectively, there are subconscious interactions between brains we are not consciously aware of but which are essential for relationships.

These connections are also critical to our well-being and happiness. According to Goleman, Empathic Accuracy, the ability to "understand" or "read" the mind of another human, can save our lives. He describes disarming an assailant with our words after understanding his motives and using this knowledge to dissuade him from a criminal act. Basically, Empathic Accuracy is the ability to put ourselves inside somebody else's shoes and to identify how and why people feel a specific way. If we were able to better understand the assailant, we may be able to get out of the situation. As you can imagine, Empathic Accuracy can have significant consequences for relationships as well. There are many variables limiting this ability and creating relationship issues.

Goleman also believes that "significant gaps in empathic understanding can be detrimental to relationships." We all have a need to feel that we're being listened to because it leads to the connectedness Brené Brown described in her TED Talk. Empathic Accuracy and understanding can be significantly enhanced with vulnerability. Goleman suggests asking "you" questions on dates versus talking about oneself to enhance this mental process.

Our neural circuitry—how we're organically wired—impacts our Empathic Accuracy and how we interact with the world. Goleman sites Harvard Psychologist Gerome Kagan, whose research indicates how kids are predisposed to specific traits at birth, like being shy, but states parents can nudge them to try new things, making them bolder. The conclusion here is that our traits and personalities can be shaped by our environment. That is no surprise to us, since we established in chapter two that our parents can have a substantial impact on our paradigms, which create our personalities. However, it helps to understand that there are biological processes at work in the formation of our paradigms as well.

Goleman also cites a 2004 study by Karen Parker, supporting the opinion that fear can have a positive impact on our emotional development. The study discovered when kids are exposed to moderate doses of fear, they'll be more well-adjusted and socially-aware adults. Again, no surprise since experiencing fear and facing it will expand their paradigms and allow them greater contextual self-awareness. As

Goleman states, however, the key is to not expose them to so much fear that it traumatizes them. We know from our work it can result in limiting beliefs and stuck paradigms.

As Goleman wrote in *Social Intelligence*: "Vitality arises from sheer human contact, especially from loving connections. This makes the people we care about almost an elixir of sorts, an ever-renewing source of energy. The neural exchange between a grandparent and a toddler, between lovers or a satisfied couple, or among good friends, has palpable virtues [. . .] the practical lesson for us all comes down to, nourish your social connections."

And yet, Goleman and other scientists warn of the potential dark side of social connections: stress (Ito and Kubota, 2021). Since there are biological functions at work based on our relationships, our stress levels, and therefore our health, can be impacted by negative relationships or interactions.

THE FREEZING SPELLS OF STAGE FRIGHT

I enjoyed my four years at Cornell University. My mind was expanded by numerous and diverse people, courses, and experiences. I was stressed and tested in all sorts of ways, and my paradigm was better for it. One specific example relating to social neuroscience occurred during my junior year.

As part of a required communications class, I had to deliver a talk to my entire class in front of around thirty fellow School of Hotel Administration classmates. I don't believe any other class created more stress and fear than this class did for me. I could handle the workload and the complexity of any academic challenge, but standing in front of an audience and speaking was way outside of my comfort zone. I don't know the source of the fear, but I had been shy my entire life. I would classify myself as more of an introvert than a social bug.

Since I was committed to academic success and there was no way around the situation, I forced myself to deliver the speech. I prepared as much as I could and it was a less than stellar performance. I froze on more than one occasion and my mind raced to the point I couldn't remember some of the facts I planned to mention about the positive impacts of coffee; I chose a subject of passion to help alleviate the fear. While I survived the ordeal, my cortisol levels—our natural alarm system, the stress hormone— reached the greatest heights of my academic career. Interestingly, though, I was part of a Latin dance group (Sabor Latino) and, even when dancing in front of hundreds of strangers as part of that crowd of performers, I never experienced stress. It was downright exhilarating.

According to Tiffany A. Ito and Jennifer T. Kubota in their online social neuroscience learning module called *The Noba Project*, "Worrying about what other people think of us is not the only source of social stress in our lives. Other research has shown that interacting with people who belong to different social groups than us—what social psychologists call 'outgroup' members—can increase physiological stress responses." On the contrary, this does not happen when interacting with "ingroup" members (people who belong to the same social group as we do). I definitely felt like an outsider in that class, but based on cultural similarities, I was comfortable within my Sabor Latino dance group.

As the authors summarized for their module, "What determines whether others will increase or decrease stress? What matters is the context of the social interaction. When it has potential to reflect badly on the self, social interaction can be stressful, but when it provides support and comfort, social interaction can protect us from the negative effects of stress."

REVOLUTIONARY SELF-EMPOWERMENT VIA MINDSIGHT

Mindsight, grounded in neuroscience and psychology, offers a revolutionary means of learning about ourselves. Understanding our Mindsight can help us change our behaviors, lead more balanced lives, and empower our paradigms.

Daniel Goleman discusses the importance of Mindsight in *Social Intelligence*. The idea is with our Mindsight, we can recognize and sense what the other person is feeling, thinking, and even intending. Our brains have cells that act like a Wi-Fi antenna and read other people automatically, without us being aware that it's going on. This sounds as difficult to believe as when Einstein was first exposed to quantum mechanics and uttered the famous words, "God does not play dice" as a way to dispose of an idea he believed preposterous.

However, even the world's top physicist, as far as I am concerned, was not up with the times on new scientific theory. Those were the early days of this theoretical science. Today, quantum mechanics, which relies on the constant appearing and disappearing of subatomic particles, is used in most advanced technological equipment, like computers and cell phones. Mindsight has the same potential to advance our paradigms and reveal our subconscious power.

Dr. Daniel Siegel, a clinical professor of psychiatry at the UCLA School of Medicine and the founding co-director of the Mindful Awareness Research Center at UCLA, is an expert on Mindsight. He is also the Executive Director of the Mindsight Institute, an educational organization that studies how the development of Mindsight can be enhanced by examining the interface of human relationships and basic biological processes.

He describes Mindsight as "the way we can focus attention on the nature of the internal world. It's how we focus our awareness on ourselves, so our own thoughts and feelings, and it's how we're able to actually focus on the internal world of someone else. So, at a very minimum, it's how we have insight into ourselves, and empathy for others" (*PsychAlive*, 2009).

This sounds a lot like the benefits of vulnerability, but what Dr. Seigel describes is more of an internal process grounded in biology. "Mindsight is more than just an understanding. Mindsight gives us the tools to monitor the internal world with more clarity and depth. And also, to modify that internal world with more power and strength. So, in all these ways Mindsight is a construct, that's a bit larger than insight, it's even larger than mindfulness because it's really about not just being present moment to moment, but it's about being present, so you monitor what's going on, but then modify what's happening."

He's effectively describing the biological infrastructure of our mental paradigms. "So, it's an empowering action-oriented way of describing the power of the mind, to actually change the structure and function of the brain that you aren't prisoner to the synaptic legacy that you had because you had these experiences that got shaped with mindset. You can actually alter the course of your life because you become awakened to the power of attention to actually integrate areas that weren't integrated before. And when we modify the internal world, we can move it from chaotic ways of being and rigid ways of being, to more harmonious function" (*PsychAlive*, 2009).

Dan Siegel has a general view of Mindsight providing us with the real source of its potential. He says Mindsight "is a way of really taking a mind and awakening it to the fact that you aren't just a passive participant in life but can be an active captain of your own ship. This is how you become the author of your own story of your life" (*PsychAlive*, 2009).

HARVARD UNIVERSITY STUDY OF ADULT DEVELOPMENT

The positive benefits of social neuroscience are attained by our selection of our close relationships. According to Robert Waldinger in his TED Talk, "What Makes a Good Life", your relationships are the key to your happiness and well-being. He's the director of the *Harvard University Study of Adult Development*, which gathered physical and mental health information from people in the Boston area for eighty years (Siegel, 2021). The findings of the study can only be described as groundbreaking.

They prove that close relationships, more than money, fame, or other perceptions of power, are what provide happiness in our journey through life. Those connections "protect people from life's discontents, help to delay mental/physical decline, and are more correlated to long and happy lives than social class, intelligence, genetics or any other factor."

What is even more interesting to me, is that those findings proved true across the board, including for the Harvard students/alumni as well as the inner-city participants not affiliated with the school. What this means is that your paradigms are heavily impacted by your close relationships, more so than almost anything else. I believe close relationships also significantly impact how we interact with ourselves. Friends offer their views of our lives, which allows us to discuss our circumstances and to expand our paradigm, gaining greater perspective.

Thus, one of the most powerful ways to positively impact your paradigm is to develop strong, long-term, positive relationships with a cross section of people. As we've discussed in a previous chapter, those with close connections are "wholehearted" people who believe in the power of vulnerability and take the type of risks leading to expanded paradigms and paradigm shifts.

Keep in mind that biases and other issues impacting your paradigm are created from interactions with other humans and society.

MARGINAL THINKING AND RELATIONSHIPS

The interdependence we create as kids leads to a lifetime of conditional or marginal thinking regarding relationships that belittles their importance. To control other people (or perhaps to subconsciously protect our emotions), we make our relationships dependent on amorphous or specific requirements based on our personal reality. We say things like, "I will not be your friend if you do this," or "I will not love you or be with you if you do that." This is a paradigmatically debilitating way to view relationships, especially when they're our top priority. Clay Christensen's Marginal Thinking principle applies especially to relationships, with yourself and others.

You cannot allow marginal or conditional thinking to invade your relationship paradigm, as it will create limiting beliefs and potentially destroy them in real life. The conditionality will apply to you as well, since relationships are mirrors. This conditionality will detrimentally impact your integrity (and thus, your authenticity), and you will not honor your word since you'll expect that the other person won't meet your conditions.

When it comes to parents, children, spouses, and close friends, be both responsible and personally accountable for your relationships fully. What I mean by this is that you should be there for your family and friends no matter what—without conditions. In a marriage, for example, make yourself 100 percent responsible for the well-being of the relationship. Respect the healthy boundaries—giving them space for personal reflection and conversations with others to cultivate their paradigms—and you have to minimize your negative emotional outputs which typically lead to attempting to control the behavior of others. Our attempt at more power or limiting others by making it fifty-fifty (or any other fraction) is a downhill slope.

None of us can operate on fractional relational responsibility. It's a sign of a relationship paradigm crisis. The minute such a rule is instituted is the beginning of relationship problems. Since our paradigms are personal, not only can we not understand when or if 50 percent has been met, but we will define it differently as well. It's a set up for failure.

However, if both people in the relationship instead make themselves (individually) 100 percent responsible for it, it'll be set up for long term success. Both will do their best to find adequate solutions to problems versus blaming the other person. Each will be more understanding when the other struggles. Each will be empathetic when necessary. A relationship is a journey, just like self-awareness. It will have ups and downs full of learning opportunities for both people. Every challenge is an opportunity to strengthen it. Furthermore, we're all struggling through our journey in life, and it is important to understand that, from an existential perspective, we are fellow travelers and we must help each other along the way.

SO WHAT DOES THIS MEAN FOR YOUR PARADIGM?

Since we live life in our own personal reality, we choose to minimize the importance of relationships and give away our power. Social neuroscience has helped us understand that true reality is a complicated web of systems that are internal and external to our paradigm but are interconnected, impacting us biologically and mentally via our relationships.

The way we impact the world is through our interactions with other people. When we act selflessly toward others, we also treat ourselves better. We reflect our kind actions to others internally. It's a renewal process. It humbles us as we realize we are all fragile and depend on others for our well-being.

Principle 11: You already do it unconsciously, so prioritize relationships above everything else and make yourself 100 percent responsible for them.

CHAPTER 12

Society, Purpose, and Meaning

"'Finding yourself' is not really how it works. You aren't a ten-dollar bill in last winter's coat pocket. You are also not lost. Your true self is right there, buried under cultural conditioning, other people's opinions, and inaccurate conclusions you drew as a kid that became your beliefs about who you are. 'Finding yourself' is actually returning to yourself. An unlearning, an excavation, a remembering who you were before the world got its hands on you."

—EMILY MCDOWELL

School Ties is a 1992 drama based on the real-life experience of Dick Wolf, the creator of the successful *Law and Order* series on NBC (Hayes, 2013). The movie is set in the 1950s and offers us a glimpse at the destructive power that prejudices and racism have on society and the individuals it impacts.

A working class Jewish student (David Greene), is offered a football scholarship to St. Matthews, an elite high school that will pave his way to Harvard. Students and staff are anti-Semitic, so he hides his background, pretending to be like them despite having a history of ardently defending his heritage.

At St. Matthews, David connects with his friend and classmate Dillon after an unfortunate incident with a fellow student. David cannot fathom that someone would go insane over a failing grade, but parental pressure to attain power and wealth are high. Dillon provides insight: "Good grades. The right schools. The right colleges, the right connections. Those are the keys to the kingdom. None of us ever goes off and lives by its wits. We do the things they tell us to do. Then they give us the good life. Hope we like it when we get it."

While I never personally felt this pressure at Cornell, I indirectly witnessed its repercussions. Cornell is notorious for having multiple students commit suicide annually because the pressure gets too high—this is the case for all Ivy League and top schools. As an example, the engineering and physics programs are world class, but the average grade is a C since the school uses a Bell Curve grading system. To be admitted, students must be at the top of their class. A C is a paradigm shift for high-performing students and their parents, especially when the average at other schools, like Princeton and Harvard, is an A-. The resulting stress is unbearable for some. Cornell is proactive about managing the situation and does a great job, but some students cannot deal with the pressure. There is only so much a school can do when control of the situation is mostly in the hands of the individual.

Dillon tells David that when he was a freshman, a student killed himself because he didn't get into Harvard. David is incredulous and Dillon responds, "I envy you [. . .]. 'Cause if you get what you want, you'll deserve it. And if you don't, you will manage. You don't have to live up to anybody else's expectations. You are who you are. That's really what draws people to you, David. It's not that you are the cool quarterback." David tries to tell him he's the most popular guy on campus, but Dillon pushes back, telling him his standing was all due to his last name and his family's favorable socioeconomic situation.

Unfortunately, many parents try to create replicas of themselves instead of giving their children the ability to find their true identity and leave their own mark in their journey of life. As a working-class student studying with privileged classmates, I never fully appreciated the pressure and stress imposed on them by parents. The desire to please parents and attain wealth and power can come at serious cost for our internal selves and society. This misplaced priority robs people of the happiness and well-being created by strong relationships, as we saw in the last chapter. I'm fortunate that my parents never pressured me to perform academically. It was my decision.

Dillon becomes infuriated with David when he goes out with Sally, on whom Dillon has had a crush for years. He finds out David is Jewish and tells other students as way to get revenge. They are appalled and want nothing to do with the cool quarterback who gave them a championship and was their close friend, all because of his religious background.

David's discussion with his close friend and roommate, Reece, is insightful. He's upset David didn't tell him that he was Jewish. "Jews are different. It's not like the difference between Methodists and Lutherans. I mean Jews . . . everything about them is different." Their open and honest dialogue expands Reece's paradigms, and he begins to defend David.

Almost everyone else turns against David, though, even Sally, who was madly in love with him prior to the revelation. She and her family are embarrassed she was dating someone Jewish, demonstrating society's acceptance of this awful bias. When she rejects him, David admits, "I didn't lie to you. I lied to my father. I lied to myself." The conversation is a mirror marking a turning point in how he deals with the situation.

David becomes fearless because he is now an outcast. He becomes willing to fight, to face his fears, and accept who he is in the face of disapproval from society. He's deemed unworthy of their friendship because he is different. When an anonymous student places a swastika over David's bed, he writes a note challenging the coward to fight, but the culprit remains incognito. Amidst this chaos, David finds his true self again.

This is just a movie, but the truth is that the emotional outputs and control that prejudice, racism, and other ills of society are experienced daily by millions of people. And this reality has significant, detrimental consequences for all of us.

The fact is that we're all prejudiced in one way, shape, or form, regardless of where we come from or what we look like. We all experience these types of feelings imposed by society, parents, and other information sources and authority figures. These limiting beliefs are exposed and informed for us to be authentic and operate above the fray.

School Ties is a powerful illustration of the chaos and issues that prejudice and other insecurities unleash on society. They create a tangled web of emotions and deceptions, denial and inauthenticity passed on from parent to child, friend to friend, and even from business and institutional leaders. The resulting hatred creates disunity and mistrust.

IMPACT OF AN INDIVIDUAL'S PARADIGM ON SOCIETY

Human interactions and relationships are the fabric of our world. They define, drive, and create society. Since our individual paradigms guide each of us, it is the sharing of our paradigms and experiences that propels humanity forward or sets it back. However, as we discussed in the last chapter, our individuality can also create a chaotic world if we allow ourselves to be led by the numerous fears we all experience/have due to our natural uniqueness/disconnection. If we grow up in a loving household, fear lies outside our family in most situations. However, if we do not, then fear is everywhere and we are trapped inside ourselves and unable to connect.

Whether for hunter-gatherer survival thinking or other reasons, humans are afraid of the unknown, of that which is different. We are uncomfortable with people or situations unfamiliar to us. We spend so many years at "home" and with our families, that by the time we are old enough to leave home or go to college, we're used to being in our comfort zones. Our immediate families define our comfort zones. Furthermore, our parents spend so much of their time protecting us and showing us how to be "safe," physically, emotionally, and financially, that we're indoctrinated in inadvertent or purposeful ways. Many times, parents just talk with each other and to their kids in manners or about subjects that can meaningfully impact their paradigms. As was discussed above, Sally Wheeler's parents clearly had a meaningful impact on her prejudice toward Jews.

Relationships are a mirror, but sometimes we don't like or are afraid of the reflection we see, consciously or subconsciously. We start with a lie that says "I am nothing like you or those people." That lie may have been implanted by a parent or another source, but it basically says "I'm better than those people," which is also a lie. The "I am not like them" mentality focuses on the judgments and/or prejudices we have, which are based on how we are different somehow (color, weight, height, religion, language, etc.). Since we're all highly unique and special beings, finding superficial differences is not hard. But the belief we are different is a lie and a surrender to fear to alleviate some internal pain. Underneath all the layers of fear, insecurity, and protection, when we remove the superficial covering, we are, at our core, exactly the same. We are born and will die alone. We're all struggling through our journey through life. We have the same needs and the same capacity for good and evil. We all share this planet and have a responsibility for it, whether we acknowledge it or not. The only meaningful characteristic that makes us truly unique is our paradigm—everything else is superficial and a judgment or opinion created by that paradigm, often based on fear.

Look in the mirror and acknowledge we have the capacity for compassion and kindness, but also for the same evil and cruelty as everyone else. Look into your mirror with blatant honesty and acknowledge that every single person you see and judge, regardless of the superficial differences, if you were in their shoes, you would be exactly like them. This would be the case if we were talking about George Washington, Gandhi, Martin Luther King, Jr., Hitler, or John Wilkes Booth. Acknowledge that despite the perceived differences, like money, socioeconomic status, skin color, and religious or other beliefs, at the core, we're all the same! We are all born free, and via our interactions with society, we develop paradigms making us who and what we believe we are.

If that is the case, who you are is just a series of interactions, experiences, and influences with other people. That is not true. You are a special being. Who you are is a person with the ability to think for yourself, expand your paradigm, and view life from a clear and logical perspective, with the ability to think and decide what you want to think and decide without undue influence. However, to operate in such an honest and genuine manner, you have to free the self that is "buried under cultural conditioning, other people's opinions, and inaccurate conclusions you drew as a kid" as stated in Emily McDowell's quote at the beginning of the chapter. It's your choice to be a wild and disorganized patchwork of society's influencers, or to be yourself. However, to be yourself takes work, proactivity, and facing your fears.

Until you are honest with yourself and acknowledge this, your fears and insecurities will be focused on being afraid, even if subconsciously, of that which makes others different. The fear will make you feel like you're better than others to alleviate your insecurity and your sensitive ego. Until you see this reality for what it is, you will continue to be self-focused and disconnected from true reality and your true self.

When you see yourself for who you truly are, you'll see others for who they truly are as well. You will have the ability to find purpose and meaning in life. Purpose and meaning can only be found via helping others. It is a genuine, authentic act connecting you with others in a powerful way. That's why, when you perform an act of kindness or a selfless act, you feel so great inside—because you connect with your true authentic self. Thus, when you help others, you help yourself. Your act is mirrored back unto you. Kindness is an acknowledgment that we're all the same. Kind people are authentic people. It's an act of love and selflessness that gets reflected back at us from the core of our being. It's beautiful and elegant.

It's natural to feel this way and to be kind to your family and those who already love you. There is less fear and risk there in most situations. However, to truly find yourself, you will have to do this when it is scary and not easy. If you do not see others for who they truly are, without fear lenses on, you won't have the capacity to help them, and thus will be unable to find real meaning and purpose in life, which lies outside of the self. Embrace the differences and realize that, while there may be risks, the door of vulnerability is more beneficial to you than you realize.

SOME IMPORTANT QUESTIONS TO CONSIDER:

- Do you have any prejudices or judgments about other people that may be detrimentally impacting your relationships and your lenses?
- Do you understand that prejudices are your fears and insecurities manifested as hatred for people who are different, and that these fears and insecurities have everything to do with you and nothing to do with other people?
- Do you know prejudices and judgments are fears that take aware your power?
- Are there any groups of people you blame for the problems or the evils of society? If so, what is at the core of this belief?

EXPANDING MY CULTURAL PARADIGM

When I was in the Dominican Republic, I had no concept of race. Dominicans come in all shapes and sizes. They can be dark-skinned or blue-eyed and blonde. It's a mixed culture comprised of European, African, and indigenous ancestors. As an example, my family is as diverse as it gets. We have the full color spectrum. One set of grandparents were Spanish immigrants, giving my mom her pale complexion and blue eyes. The other set are mixed with my grandmother, looking like what someone from Ghana looks like. As a result, my father is mixed and so am I. I can pass for Middle Eastern, Indian, South American, Sicilian Italian, and a bunch of races whose people have olive skin. There are many color spectrums in the Dominican Republic. Growing up with this rich diversity all around me, I did not understand racial prejudices. I had people of all possible skin colors who loved me and whom I love. My parents displayed no preference to one or another.

However, when I was brought to this country, the prejudices of society were imposed on my paradigm for the first time. New York City television networks painted a dangerous city full of violent criminals. Most of the criminals portrayed were African American men. In my innocent nine-year-old brain, these "criminals" posed a danger to my mother since we lived in a "dangerous" neighborhood. Thus, I accompanied her everywhere she went to protect her. I worried "they" would hurt my mother. Now that I have an expanded paradigm on the subject, it pains me to know I was subjected to this type of societal brainwashing. I was fortunate to have numerous other experiences that expanded my paradigm to understand the beauty of our differences versus fearing them.

Not that there wasn't violence in New York City in the 1980s, but the networks were clearly racist in their misrepresentation of the problems of society as well as who was responsible for them. I figured that out based on my exposure to African Americans in my neighborhood. Our superintendent was an African American man named Butch. My father liked and trusted him. He was helpful to our family, treated us with dignity and respect, and he was genuinely nice to my siblings and me. We lived in an old rent-controlled building and there were frequent problems with plumbing and/or heating. Butch was always there for us, day or night.

A few months after I came to the US, my father asked me to get Butch to fix something. I don't recall the specifics of the issue that day. It may have been the first time I ever went out of our apartment alone. Butch lived in the same block, some three hundred yards north on Norfolk Street.

I knocked on the door of a third-floor apartment and Butch opened the door. His father and some other family members were there. For reasons I did not understand, his father screamed at him to "get that darned kid out of here."

Rushing me out, Butch was embarrassed and apologetic. We spoke on the way back to my apartment. The conversation gave me some insights into both his dad and the struggles of African Americans in the US. Butch's dad had a difficult life based on the impacts of race relations in this country. This was my first exposure to American history and our extensive racial injustices.

I started to see the news with different eyes. African Americans were no longer the dangerous criminals the networks wanted me to see. They were my superintendent and his family. I didn't have any African American classmates at the time; there weren't any at my school that I can remember. The first time I met and interacted with African Americans of a similar age was in high school. They became my close friends and my fellow wrestling team members. In college, I decided to live in Ujamaa, a residence hall at Cornell University's north campus that celebrates the rich and diverse heritage of black people in the United States, Africa, the Caribbean, and other regions of the world. The experience further expanded my perspective on African Americans.

Today I have close friends of numerous different races. I am grateful I can see the world through their eyes when we speak and spend time together. I believe one of the greatest gifts to humanity was the creation of distinct people who look different and see the world from a unique perspective. Such rich diversity is both elegant and expands our paradigms. It makes us a stronger and more powerful society.

HOW IS SOCIETY'S PARADIGM CREATED?

What was obvious in *School Ties* is that the antisemitic sentiments of the students came directly from the parents or from the other students. Prejudices, judgments, assumptions, and other hateful opinions about other people or races are transferred via conversations with others. As a matter of fact, the rules, norms, and prejudices of society are all created and shared via conversations, discussions, and collaborations by humans. That's how society functions. The majority of society, and more likely the key influencers (those with power), share their opinions and shape the conversations, paradigms, and feelings of the rest of that specific group being influenced. Many people start off by simply being spectators in the discussion, but eventually become part of the conversation.

These negative emotional outputs (racism, prejudices, etc.) always provide the influencers with some type of material or other (perceived) benefit. Regarding racism, it's a feeling of superiority that addresses an internal feeling of inferiority to others, the feeling that says, "I am not good enough." As an example, when Africans were stolen from their country and sold to early Americans as slaves, the rationalization was that they were less civilized, less educated, and inferior based on the color of their skin, religion, or any number of reasons. However, the benefit of free labor and the creation and accumulation of wealth, in addition to the addictive feeling of superiority to another human, must have been quite enticing as well.

Despite the absolutely horrific, unjust, immoral, and savage treatment of these amazing humans, the majority of American society and the world accepted the situation. The influencers at the time had the power, and those who believed it was wrong were complicit by their silence and lack of effort to right the wrong. It was easier for all of society to be numb and disconnected from the suffering of millions of African Americans so they could live with themselves. However, their stuck paradigms had detrimental societal consequences.

The abolition of slavery manifested from a few principled people in power. The effort required continuous, slow progress from those with moral underpinnings in the face of hatred, who risked their lives to make progress. It was a major act of courage, which even resulted in the killing of Abraham Lincoln and countless others.

What do you think is the true source of racism and other hateful feelings? As Reece said in *School Ties*, the simple fact of being different is what created his dislike for Jews. Being different, and the extensive fear that it creates, is what has separated people and societies for millennia. When there's a distinction, there is an opportunity for one person, group, gender, race, or species to be more powerful than the other. And since this is correlated to our mirrors, the desire for power reflects an attempt to hide self-hatred and mitigate deep-seeded insecurity.

Furthermore, when two groups are created, the influencers doing so, regardless of how unlovable they really are, all of a sudden have a group they belong to—one where they have a special role. Thus, they solve their inability to connect to others because they're unable to be vulnerable from their fear of disconnection. It's a major selfish ego play that satisfies a feeling of inferiority.

As humans and citizens, we have a responsibility to make sure we're acting on behalf of our planet and the rest of the people of our society. We shouldn't simply mindlessly agree, enable, or become complicit in what our leaders are doing. We have enough information to understand the corruptible nature of power from what our history books tell us. Whether it's slavery, poverty created by low salaries, or some other form of oppression, every society has an elite minority that benefits from the silence, complicity, or naivete of the majority, which, despite having most of the power, give it away and become numb to the evils of society in the same manner that our paradigms do.

This happens because one or more individuals are executing a societal paradigm shift to make you see and live their reality. They don't want you to have your own voice, but to make their goals come true. You can clearly see and understand how this happened throughout history, such as in Germany when Hitler was in power, or in the US during slavery and during the killing and genocide of indigenous inhabitants of this country, or during Apartheid in Africa.

Stuck paradigms have a huge capacity for evil, selfishness, and power hunger. Hitler and Stalin are not larger-than-life people. They were not acting in the best interest of their citizens. These were people with major fears and insecurities allowed by large populations to kill millions of other people. Do you believe you would have done anything to prevent the evils they unleashed if you had been there? What could you have done? Would you have cared? How are those sentiments reflected in your daily actions today?

HITLER VS. MARTIN LUTHER KING, JR.

Adolf Hitler and Martin Luther King, Jr. represent two massively distinct paradigms. One paradigm was very stuck and self-focused, the other highly expanded and selfless. Both had tremendous impacts on society and influenced millions of people.

ADOLF HITLER

Adolf Hitler's deep seated and unexplored feelings of "I am not worthy" led to stuck paradigms and a complete burial of his true self/reality, resulting in the murder of millions of Jews as well as global warfare. His father worked for the customs office in Vienna and wanted his son to follow in his footsteps (Kershaw, 2008). However, both were strong-willed and a rivalry developed that destroyed their relationship (Keller, 2010). Hitler was fond of painting and wanted to attend a classical high school where he could become an artist. His father disapproved. Instead, he sent him to a traditional German technical high school, a decision Hitler strenuously disagreed with (Kershaw, 2008). In *Meinkampf*,

Hitler says he rebelled against this decision and intentionally under-performed so his father would allow him to pursue his dreams. This may be true, but his constant string of failures may demonstrate otherwise. Hitler applied twice and was twice rejected from The Academy of Fine Arts (Bullock, 1962).

Instead of the hopeless suicide by Neil in *Dead Poets' Society*, Hitler gave in to his emotional outputs and set out not to find his authentic self, but feed a major sense of inadequacy. One that could never be satisfied with external pursuits. Like Neil, Hitler was deathly afraid of his father. Instead of having the courage to have a vulnerable discussion about his desired to attend artistic high school, he tried to manipulate the situation by sabotaging his father's plans for him. This level of inauthenticity corrupted his paradigm and unleashed his deep-seeded self-hatred into the external world.

Hitler's struggles were exacerbated when he became an orphan. His mother died when he was fourteen and his father when he was eighteen (Kershaw, 2008/Bullock, 1999). He had no money and basically became homeless, surviving as a laborer and selling landscape watercolors (Hitler, 1999). He attended art college but failed. He tried to be a struggling artist and also failed. Basically, he failed at his dream of becoming an artist and couldn't blame his father. It was likely this steady stream of unfaced failures that attracted him to both antisemitism and the military, since both offered feelings of power and authority that fed his distraught ego.

German nationalism had a strong following where he lived, and the proliferated prejudicial sentiments played on Christians' fear related to the numerous Jewish Eastern European immigrants (Hamann, 2010/Hitler, 1999). Hitler read many of the publications at the time which fanned the flames of racism and hatred, most of which were authored by politicians expressing German nationalism (Hamann, 2010). Initially deemed unfit for service, Hitler found his calling and much success in the military (Kershaw, 1999). "He greeted the war with enthusiasm, as a great relief from the frustration and aimlessness of civilian life. He found discipline and comradeship satisfying and was confirmed in his belief in the heroic virtues of war" (*Encyclopedia Britannica Online*, 2021).

At a time of strong German nationalism, Hitler offered many citizens a powerful and potent feeling that united them around him: hate. Hate is a vigorous and self-serving feeling that gives the recipient a false sense of superiority over the people they despise. It is based on fear and the deep-seated feeling of inferiority versus that person or group. Hatred of the Jews essentially allowed a struggling and impoverished citizenry a feeling of superiority over another race because they were different. It gave them the intoxicating feeling of power. This powerful weapon is the one Hitler weaponized to brainwash people and rise to power. He used conversations, speeches, writings, and his oratory skills to brainwash citizens who accepted his blissful "blue pill."

The Holocaust and other multiplier effects of this hatred, as well as the resulting negative societal paradigm shift that occurred, will haunt humanity for centuries.

MARTIN LUTHER KING, JR.

Martin Luther King, Jr. executed a societal paradigm shift that saved millions of lives and allowed people from two races to unite. As is the case with all paradigm expansions and shifts, he did so by engaging in a public dialogue not only with African Americas, but with the United States of America. He painted a picture of love and unity in society based on morality, ethics, and fairness. Despite the great injustice, his discourse was civil, though uncompromising. Martin Luther King, Jr. expanded his paradigm many times throughout his life and had many opportunities to understand the benefits and possibility of the dream he was manifesting. As an example, he was pleasantly surprised by the fact that African Americans were not segregated and lived together in peace during his trip to Connecticut prior to starting college. He also had been in love with a white woman when in seminary.

More importantly, he had a moral foundation developed since birth centered on ethics, fairness, and principles. His paradigm was expanded after numerous failures and struggles, and he could see reality, which allowed him to understand the meaning and impact of his actions. He was acting in the best interest of society and understood that he was putting his life at risk to achieve his definition of success. He empowered millions of African Americans and expanded the paradigms of millions of white people who were allowed to live a more ethical and morally-centered way of life with a better understanding of right and wrong. Society doesn't speak much about his impact on white people. He freed them from mental slavery, which allowed them to think segregation and the enslavement of a group of people was justified. There's so much power in that if you think of the removal of hatred, prejudice, and mistrust just because someone is different. The expansion of a paradigm from a principle-centered perspective is a powerful manifestation.

There's also an incredible multiplier effect to Martin Luther King, Jr.'s actions that we don't speak of enough, as if we take it for granted. There are literally millions of African American people in the US and people of color in the world who have been able to manifest their idea of success because of his gift of the power of an expanded paradigm. Can you imagine the limiting beliefs that being black in a Jim Crow, separated South would manifest on the children of former slaves? I feel as if Martin Luther King, Jr.'s dream was multiplied. People of color can dream and set out to accomplish anything they want in today's US. Whites and blacks, instead of being segregated, are united to add meaningful value to society. It is clear that the impact of this on society is invaluable.

Sure, many obstacles remain; the fight is not yet over, but the major limits have been removed. It's no longer illegal to attend any college for a person of color or pursue any desired achievement. If you are a person of color, you have a responsibility not only to continue this multiplier effect, but to ensure the dream is fully realized. If you are white, you have the benefit of you and your children living in a free, more advanced society. The rewards are greater than you can imagine and flow from the diverse perspectives, collective intelligence, culture, music, and business achievements of our society.

What's the purpose of society, and what are the extremes we witness? What's the purpose of good and evil? If you are an active and involved observer and player in the game of life, the differences in society open your eyes to choices. You can choose good, or you can choose evil. You can define yourself and your purpose. You can choose a "blue pill" and live a meaningless and blissful existence clouded by naivete, or you can take a "red pill" and realize the purpose of life is to find purpose in life—to make it count. Life is too precious and unique to live up to 120 years without making a mark on humanity, or at least one person's life. As Pablo Picasso said, "The meaning of life is to find your gift. The purpose of life is to give it away."

SO WHAT DOES THIS MEAN FOR YOUR PARADIGM?

You pass your paradigms down to your kids and potentially to any person with whom you have a conversation. Regardless of who you are, you're an influencer to someone, even if they don't tell you. As humans, we have a great responsibility to expand our paradigms and help our fellow humans, especially those with stuck paradigms who are enslaved to their fears and don't see reality with clear lenses. We also have a responsibility to ensure runaway egos and people with massive insecurities, such as Hitler, are not in power and leading society to commit horrible atrocities. We have a tremendous amount of power, and it's our responsibility to use it. If we don't, we are complicit in the evils of society. As a result, we must work on our paradigms constantly and understand the amount of power they give us.

The multiplier effect of hate and by successive generations is still evident today. America is still fighting a war against racism and oppression. This topic continues dividing us. So, what can you do as an individual? Vote, become a politician, a journalist, or otherwise bring awareness to specific topics, like Greta Thunberg meaningfully shifted the global paradigm on climate change. Most importantly, expand your paradigm, and do not allow leaders and influencers to divide you and create an "us versus them," mentality—that's how they get power and take away yours. And remember, there's a multiplier effect to your decisions.

Principle 12: Create goals and make a difference to society. Lead yourself and others to create a better world. Wake others up, like Neo and Morpheus. Join the quest to create a better world.

CHAPTER 13

Renewal and other Paradigmatic Necessities

———

"Change is supremely inconvenient, uncomfortable, and naturally scary. Yet we only move through life through the process of change, reinvention and renewal, and so bravery is our quintessential rebel for pushing us past our own limiting beliefs and behaviors. Bravery is feeling the fear, immersing yourself into it and through it so you can come out the other side."

—CHRISTINE EVANGELOU

The Shack is a powerful and difficult movie about paradigmatic renewal through the eyes of a broken man disconnected from reality. Though the movie is created from the worldview and principles of Christianity, it can easily be viewed from a self-reflection perspective as well. The man is forced to deal with his traumatic issues and free himself from stuck paradigms that impact not only him, but the rest of his family.

The Phillips family appear to be a happy, connected, and deeply religious family, but McKenzie, the father, is broken inside based on trauma suffered as a child.

McKenzie has limiting beliefs and blames God for the physical abuse he and his mother endured at the hands of his alcoholic father, who was a minister.

A present day tragedy destroys the family. During a camping trip, his youngest daughter is kidnapped and murdered; they find her blood and dress in a shack in the woods. The kids become disconnected from reality, with the son lying and sneaking out of the house and finding ways to cope externally. The other daughter becomes inwardly focused, unable to socialize because she blames herself for her sister's death. The mother is better than the rest based on her relationship with God, spirituality, and trust that life is ultimately fair.

McKenzie is in too much despair to see outside of his reality and try to help his loved ones. He is suicidal, full of hatred, and disconnected from the real world. He exists but is numb to reality because of the weight of his pain and his inability to move past his trauma. He blames God for allowing this tragedy to happen. How can God be so unfair and allow so much evil in the world?

He receives a letter asking him to meet "Papa" at the scene of his daughter's murder, a shack in the woods. He does not know if it is a joke, or correspondence from the murderer trying to draw him back to kill him, but he decides to go and face his fear. When he realizes the shack is empty, he sobs at the memory of his daughter and almost shoots himself.

The wintry landscape transforms to beautiful spring scenery as he follows a Mediterranean-looking man who calls him by name. Realizing the man is Jesus Christ, he also meets God the Father ("Papa") in the form of his friendly childhood neighbor, as well as a young Asian woman who is the Holy Spirit ("Sarayu").

"Why did you bring me here?" he asks God. "Because here is where you got stuck," Papa replied. "I want to heal that wound that is growing inside you and between us. There is no easy answer that will take the pain away. No instant fix that is enduring. Life takes a bit of time and a lot of relationship." McKenzie accuses her of abandoning his daughter and asks where she was when he needed her most. Papa answers, "Son, when all you see is your pain, you lose sight of me." In other words, when we view our lives from a stuck paradigm, we are not in sync with reality and we filter life through our emotional pain, a place of weakness, versus our reason and expanded paradigm that gives us power.

During the next few days, McKenzie has a lot of discussions with Papa, Sarayu, and Jesus, which allow him to reflect upon his life and reality. He is told that even though he wants the promise of a pain-free life, there isn't one. "As long as there is another (free) will in this universe, free not to follow God, evil can find a way in." He also learns his stuck paradigms rob him of joy and cripple his capacity to love, and they are trapped because he chooses not to be vulnerable since "the truth sets everyone free."

One of Mack's conversations with Sarayu is particularly revealing. It explains why life is so complicated for humanity from a paradigmatic perspective. We all want to control life, but a whole world exists of people with different perspectives that can create chaos. Sarayu helps Mack understand that good and evil are specific to each person's paradigm and normally is a selfish definition. We tend to define that which is bad for us as evil, even when it is not. As a result, chaos ensues.

Sarayu enlightens him: "And there are billions like you. Each determining what you think is good and evil. And when your good clashes with your neighbors' evil, arguments ensue. Wars break out. Because all insist on playing God. You weren't meant to do any of that all on your own. This was always meant to be a conversation between friends."

During his visit with God, Mack's eyes are opened to the fact that he has been unfair and blamed God based on his incomplete paradigm. God helps him understand, explore, and forgive the murderer of his daughter, a painful and powerful process that renews his paradigm and allows him to heal the pain and hurt within himself. This process changes how he sees life, and he's finally able to access reality without painful lenses. When he returns home, he is then able to truly connect with his children and help them understand, process, and forgive their pain. Mack now sees reality and isn't blinded by his own stuck paradigms, judgments, and limiting beliefs.

EXPANDING MY PARADIGM ON THE HBS EXPERIENCE

In the introduction to this book, I spoke about the feeling of betrayal that consumed me when HBS Alumni Clubs asked me to step down from an organization I founded and to which I devoted four years of my life. There's no doubt in my mind I was treated unfairly by a leader who worked for an institution I love—that was obvious to me. It is just the plain truth. However, the resulting loss of power had more to do with what was within me than anything that anyone at HBS did.

The experience allowed my internal sensors to tell me something was wrong and I needed to search within myself to understand what it was. It manifested as a loss of power and a desire to have more meaning and purpose in my life. All of this happened subconsciously, as I did not understand what was happening to me. The best way I can describe it after the fact is that I felt hurt by HBS, and the emotional pain indicated there was something awry internally. Have you ever hurt yourself physically and not realized it only to discover, via a sense of pain later, that you have an actual injury?

My career at that time was not fulfilling. I worked at a place where the only goal was pecuniary in nature, which did not sit well with me. My work for the HBS Real Estate Alumni Association allowed me to help people and produced a feeling of making a difference in the lives of others. When that was taken away, it created an imbalance that forced me to look inside myself for purpose and meaning. During this time, I also had young children, and the transition from no kids to having dependents also has a way of re-prioritizing your life. After a lot of soul searching and discussions with all sorts of people, what I realized was that I needed renewal of my paradigms and priorities:

- I needed to make a difference in the lives of others to feel like my life had meaning and purpose.
- I had already realized my goal of succeeding academically and positioning myself for professional success to get out of poverty, a goal I set out to achieve in middle school. After attending Cornell University and Harvard Business School, I had accomplished my goal of using education as a bridge to success. Thus, I needed to redefine my idea of success, and to focus on a new life challenge to strive for—another mountain needed to be climbed.
- I wanted my career to do more than generate material wealth. Helping others was a required part of my mandate, so I founded ventures that allowed me to combine my professional experience with helping society to bring more meaning into my profession.

Basically, the HBS experience resulted in a need for me to renew my paradigm and led to me working to develop greater self-awareness so I could understand why I had lost my power. I believe I am better for having gone through that experience. Whereas I felt betrayed by the school, I now feel gratitude for the journey since it allowed me to become my better self. It was not a fun or easy process, but I believe it was a productive and necessary one.

The resulting self-awareness allowed me to pursue professional and personal efforts more purposefully. Since the Harvard Business School Real Estate Alumni Association completely died, I founded The Crimson Connection in 2020 to continue my efforts to serve alumni, but in a manner not affiliated with HBS. The Crimson Connection has created numerous webinars and opportunities for alumni to learn from each other, network, exchange ideas, and interact. We have added professionals from other real estate programs to maximize our impact, including MIT, Columbia Business School, Stanford, Cornell, and University of Texas, among numerous others. To add more meaning to our efforts, the organization donates all proceeds to worthwhile nonprofit organizations. Teaching Matters, an excellent nonprofit focused on improving education for underrepresented and historically marginalized students, for which I now serve as Chairman of the Board, has received substantial donations from The Crimson Connection thanks to the generosity of its network.

I also founded Crimson Rock Capital in 2014, a real estate investment firm focusing on value add investment opportunities that have a strong combination of financial and social return. We invest in emerging locations and assets where we can be a significant catalyst for growth and transformation. As an example, in 2014 we invested in multiple hotels in New Orleans to help the city's economy recover from the detrimental impacts of Hurricane Katrina. We are currently renovating and repositioning an old hotel in disrepair in Cleveland's Midtown District that will create numerous jobs and serve as a catalyst for the revival of the area.

I co-founded Sojourner Glamping in 2020 in partnership with Andrew Murphy, my friend and HBS classmate, to add significant value to guests and rural communities in the US and, eventually, around the world. Andy has worked for The Peace Corps, World Wildlife Fund, and the Philadelphia Zoo, in addition to other for-profit roles. Most recently, he created Zaina Lodge, the highest-rated resort in Ghana and the first in West Africa to add value for local tribes. We are partnering to scale our impact by creating luxury glamping resorts that add significant value to guests, local communities, and investors while being environmentally sustainable. Our resorts will offer our guests well-being and renewal in beautiful, natural settings outside of major metropolitan areas.

I have also continued to volunteer for Harvard University and Harvard Business School over the past few years. I enjoyed a six-year term as a board member for the Harvard Club of New York where, among other efforts, I advocated for making the organization more affordable to alumni working in nonprofit organizations or in public service, such as teachers and police officers. I am also a board member for the Harvard Business School Club of New York, an organization that adds significant value to society, including helping NYC nonprofits and providing college scholarships to needy students, in addition to its numerous offerings to alumni. My interaction with the school and its organizations is more purposeful and empathetic based on my experience.

My renewed and expanded paradigm has allowed me to add more value to society, and it all started with being forced to truly look at myself in the mirror. I am enjoying my life journey much more now that I have greater self-awareness and am working on cultivating my paradigm.

RENEWAL

Renewal is a popular term these days, but most of the time, people are referring to physical aspects of renewal, which are important but incomplete. The rest of the time, people are referring to the emotional aspects. However, the ability to combine those two with also renewing your paradigm can give you constant access to power, and help you create the balance required to live a fulfilling life. Your paradigms are stuck because they need renewal, which requires you to face your fears and connect vulnerably with other humans often. We create fears all the time and renewal is necessary to stay at the top of our game.

True renewal requires you to do what you believe is uncomfortable, especially regarding your paradigm. It's not meant to be easy but transformational, which requires addressing difficult issues and conversations. Transformations disrupt the status quo to return to a new beginning. Renewal is the process by which you gain and maintain self-awareness, expand your paradigm, and access reality without clouded lenses. They are the guideposts of your self-awareness journey.

All renewal processes are essential, connected, and required for a truly balanced life. I believe there are three types of renewals necessary to have a balanced life where you are powerful and have the ability to access reality without murky lenses: physical, emotional, and paradigmatic.

Paradigmatic  Physical

Renewal

Emotional

PHYSICAL RENEWAL = PHYSICAL SELF MIRRORS

There are numerous ways to renew the physical human body, but I'll focus on those I believe are most essential. Your sleep, diet, exercise, and fun all have an impact on your paradigms, directly or indirectly.

SLEEP:

The human body is in constant need of renewal for proper function and to stay alive. We constantly renew the amount of air in our bodies through breathing and the amount of water via eating/drinking, which in turn replenishes cells in our body. Some of these physical processes seem routine, but they're critical to your overall physical, emotional, and paradigmatic functions. According to Wendy M. Troxel PhD, "Making sound decisions, being in a good mood most of the time, reining in some of your bad moods or irritability, problem solving, communicating effectively, tolerating frustration, practicing empathy—these are all important skills for cultivating and maintaining a healthy relationship. And these are also all the things that go south when you're low on sleep." I have extensive self-awareness when it comes to sleep. One of my secrets to success has been maintaining proper sleep routines and prioritizing the number of hours I sleep every night. However, while I knew sleep impacted my academic performance, I was not aware of the critical nature of the process for my relationships, emotions, and self-awareness until I began my journey of self-discovery. My key goal was to focus and excel academically, but I received substantially more benefits.

EXERCISE:
While most of us exercise because we're trying to look a certain way, the benefits of working out also include mental and emotional health, which in turn impact your paradigms. According to award-winning psychologist Ron Friedman, PhD in his *Harvard Business Review* article, "Over the past decade, social scientists have quietly amassed compelling evidence suggesting that there's another, more immediate benefit of regular exercise: its impact on the way we think. Studies indicate that our mental firepower is directly linked to our physical regimen." Ron Friedman is correlating working out with greater productivity at work, but it goes further than that. Working out can improve your paradigms and increase the productivity of your life. After trying numerous exercise routines in my life, my exercise of choice is Brazilian Jiu Jitsu (BJJ). It's a humbling sport that requires continuous learning (takes about ten years to get a black belt), focus, and effort, and is an intense workout that offers a diverse

community of practitioners. I didn't expect to meet such a diverse group of people that would expand my paradigm in so many ways. While I started my BJJ journey with a focus on exercise and health, I have gotten so much more out of the relationship, from an emotional and mental health aspect. I literally walk out of class most days feeling like I am floating in the air. I have commented many times that BJJ has made me a better father, husband, and friend.

DIET:

Interestingly, eating healthy also has an impact on our emotions/moods, in addition to how it makes us look on the outside and keeps us physically healthy. According to Eva Selhub, MD on her health blog for Harvard Medical School, "What you eat directly affects the structure and function of your brain and, ultimately, your mood. Serotonin is a neurotransmitter that helps regulate sleep and appetite, mediate moods, and inhibit pain. Since about 95 percent of your serotonin is produced in your gastrointestinal tract, and your gastrointestinal tract is lined with a hundred million nerve cells, or neurons, it makes sense that the inner workings of your digestive system don't just help you digest food, but also guide your emotions." She says that to get the benefits though, get a premium diet consisting of healthy foods void of processed and refined foods and sugars.

WORK LIFE BALANCE—PLAY/FUN/PLEASURE:

Our paradigms can also be expanded and renewed by having fun and engaging in activities that bring us pleasure, especially if we experience them with other people. Having fun, letting loose, and relaxing create balance in your live that restores energy and mood, helping you appreciate your life and relationships more. According to Julie Scharper in her *Johns Hopkins Magazine* article, "It's easy to see the evolutionary benefits of exercise triggering the brain's pleasure center. Natural selection would seem to favor animals and humans who get a buzz out of chasing prey or running away from predators. Likewise, it's clear why eating, drinking, and having sex would bring us pleasure. But why do we enjoy activities that are not clearly tied to survival or the propagation of the species? Most people find learning, creating art, exploring new places, and performing charitable acts deeply pleasurable."

According to David J. Linden, author of the book *The Compass of Pleasure*, "What's happened in humans is a miracle. Not only can humans take pleasure from things that have no relation to getting genes to the next generation, but we can take pleasure from things like fasting and celibacy, acts that run counter to the evolutionary imperative." Julie Scharper suspects that "these pleasurable activities could all be seen as a form of play. And play might just be the most important act we can engage in" (Scharper, 2016). However, what may really be going on, in my opinion, is that our paradigms decide what's pleasurable or not, and to a significant extent, we can determine the activities that will bring us balance based on the meaning and purpose they bring to our lives. Thus, renewal in the form of experiencing pleasure to create a healthy work-life balance will be a personal experience that you will discover through your self-awareness process. The key is to ensure you are aware that you should be engaging in pleasurable activities to optimize your balance and your life.

BELOW ARE SOME KEY QUESTIONS TO ASK YOURSELF IN RELATION TO YOUR PHYSICAL MIRROR:

- Do you sleep enough? If no, why not? Is sleeping enough a priority for you?
- Are you happy with the way you physically look? Why or why not?
- Do you eat healthy? Why or why not?
- How do you feel after you eat or after you work out? Does the food or type of workout matter for your mood?
- Are you eating for health, for taste, or because of stress?
- Do you have a specific diet that you follow?
- Do you have a regular exercise schedule?

EMOTIONAL RENEWAL = RELATIONSHIP RENEWAL = INTERNAL AND EXTERNAL MIRRORS

The key ingredient in emotional balance is communication with yourself and others. Emotions are tricky because you may feel a certain way and not fully understand it at first. There have been many times I felt either generally upset or upset at someone specifically and had limited awareness of it, though I would display it emotionally. Sometimes it could be a thought, idea, or judgment lurking in the back of your brain that you need to discuss and expose so you can bring awareness to your feeling. Think of that feeling of being upset (or any other emotion) as a sensor telling you that you need to bring awareness to it by discussing it. Conversation is a must for self-awareness of your emotions and the journey through it would be incomplete without it. The other key ingredient is vulnerability. Thus, to properly manage your emotions, commit to your self-awareness journey and be willing to honestly discuss your feelings with both yourself and others. You can do a lot of damage if you don't do this. Since most humans don't have self-awareness and do not follow this process, opting instead to simply react to their emotions, we cause a lot of pain and trauma. Most humans are emotionally out of balance and require renewal.

As humans we can be upset with ourselves or with others. As we have learned in this book, relationships are mirrors, and we tend to treat people as they treat us. As a result, if you do something you feel sorry about doing, it's critical you are forgiving to yourself so you can be forgiving with others. We operate with a sense of internal/external balance—that's where the mirror aspect of our personality operates. If we feel loved, we will give love. If people are forgiving toward us, we tend to be more forgiving. If someone does something that bothers us and says they are sorry, we're more likely to do the same. What this means is if we're proactive and take the first step in these situations by being forgiving, loving, and honest with ourselves, we will create the same habits with our friends and family. Do you realize the amount of power in the choices you have? You can literally influence how your friends and family treat you and create emotional balance for yourself and those you love via leading by example. First be kind and forgiving to yourself, and then to your friends and family. This will make you feel powerful not only because you're doing something kind for yourself, but because you would be emotionally uplifting for people whom you love.

BELOW ARE SOME KEY QUESTIONS TO ASK YOURSELF IN RELATION TO YOUR EMOTIONAL MIRROR:

- Whom are you most grateful for in your life?
- What are your biggest regrets?

- What are your biggest accomplishments? What are you the proudest of yourself for?
- Do you have any friends you need to reconnect with?
- Do you owe any friends/family an apology?

PARADIGMATIC RENEWAL = SELF RENEWAL = INTERNAL MIRROR

The most difficult process to renew and the most beneficial to your life and those of the people you love (and society) is your paradigmatic renewal. It's the type of process that will disrupt who you are at your core and create a metamorphosis that will meaningfully empower you—if done correctly. It is also scary, but fear is a key ingredient for this process, as is your willingness to face it. This entire book is about renewing your paradigms.

The first step is to have awareness of your paradigms and the fact that they're an accumulation of your thoughts and experiences, and they create your emotions and your reality. As I mentioned in the beginning of the book, a paradigm is not simply your mindset or an outward facing perspective, but your entire programming all in one place, meaning it is critical and essential to how you operate, how you see life, and how you process your emotions. While it is a part of you, though, it is not you, which means you control it with the choices that you make. To have awareness of it and positively impact your paradigm is a choice, as is proactively managing your paradigm so you can live a fruitful, productive, and meaningful life. Because your programming changes with your experiences, thoughts, and conversations, renewal is an essential part of maintaining self-awareness and balanced paradigms. Make balancing paradigms and renewals part of your self-improvement journey. This requires being proactive and prioritizing the cultivation of your paradigm, like a garden that must be cared for, else it will run wild.

BELOW ARE SOME KEY QUESTIONS TO ASK YOURSELF IN RELATION TO YOUR PARADIGMATIC MIRROR:

- Are you happy with life? Why or why not?
- Does your life have meaning and purpose? Why or why not?
- Why are you here on earth?
- Is life fair? Why or why not?
- Frequently answer Caroline McHugh's question: "Who do you think you are?"
- What moral and ethical principles will you live by? How do you proactively decide and then execute on them?

- What are you biggest fears? How are they holding you back? What do you need to face them?
- Are you able to honor your word? If not, why not? Commit to doing so and forgive yourself when you fail, but hold yourself accountable. There should be repercussions you can measure.

"You are in danger of living a live so comfortable and soft, that you will die without ever realizing your true potential."

—DAVID GOGGINS

SO WHAT DOES THIS MEAN FOR YOUR PARADIGM?

From physical, emotional, and paradigmatic perspectives, we need to go through renewal processes frequently to achieve the necessary balance for accessing reality without clouded lenses. Humans have a tendency to burnout in one or more of these areas, particularly paradigms, but the truth is that all of the three processes are interconnected and related. We have to work on all of them, for example, to understand and control our emotions, which impact our paradigms and our physical health. Just like self-awareness, renewal requires proactivity and balance, and is an essential ingredient in your journey of self-discovery.

Balance is required to ensure your paradigm operates in reality. Feed your mind violent movies, for example, and you'll create a violent paradigm, eventually. Feed it racist ideology and you will create a racist, stuck paradigm. The mind reaches a tipping point—after many repetitions of the same ideology, your paradigm will get stuck. Have you ever not liked a song, but after being forced to hear it many times, you end up really liking it? Repetition programs your paradigms. After you program your paradigm, your reality is altered and your paradigm could be stuck. To go back to being unstuck will require undoing the process and expanding it to the point where you're able to consciously balance out the perspective.

Furthermore, you'll have to decide to get it unstuck and create a process to do so. This sounds easy, but it requires self-awareness, which, as we have learned, 85 to 90 percent of people do not have. How many racist people do you know who changed their mind on the subject? It is a proactive, thoughtful process, and a difficult paradigm to expand.

This book is about paradigms. Paradigms require us to have self-awareness, and to keep both fresh, you need physical, emotional, and paradigmatic renewal. Life is a journey, and any and every experience will add to our programming, thus having the ability to expand our paradigms. Every single process in life, every single being in life, and your paradigms and relationships need renewal to function optimally. Exercising, eating a healthy diet, and facing your fears are not always pleasant activities, but they enable better relationships with yourself and others, the ability to access reality, and a purposeful life. To have a great looking body, you must work out. To have a healthy body, you must eat healthy foods. And to have the right mental programming, you must do both as well as engage in paradigmatic renewal, often. The amount of personal power and meaning you'll get from making this part of your journey will make it worth it!

You will have off days, but don't allow a downward spiral—don't numb yourself. Stay true to yourself and stay awake and accessing reality. Don't accept the "blue pills" of blissful naivete. You, your loved ones, and the world need you to create greater balance in yourself and society!

Self-awareness, authenticity, and adequate cultivation of your paradigm are developed through continuous effort and require significant trial and error. As Lao Tzu said, "The journey of a thousand miles begins with one step," which, when paired with the popular Chinese proverb, "The man who removes a mountain begins by carrying away small stones," shows us how this seemingly formidable task can be completed by anyone. However, the second most important take away after deciding to cultivate your paradigm is the fact that progress will be incremental and, sometimes, slow or even negative. Rough spots along the way may produce regression toward inauthenticity, and they must be viewed as great learning opportunities. Having close, critical friends and being open about setbacks will help promote forward progress.

The universe has been conspiring for you to be right here, right now. It will be transformational for you to decide to take control of your life, your feelings, your goals, and your journey! Do it for yourself, your family, and your progenitors!

Principle 13: Ensuring continuous renewal, balance, and diversity of your paradigms is key to their expansion and preventing them from getting stuck.

Acknowledgments

As my book attempts to describe, we all struggle and get lost in our journey through life at times. That is the human condition and I believe it's by intelligent design. Our struggles and the need to rely on other humans for help, comfort, support, love, and enjoyment are important seeds of opportunity. We must cultivate those seeds so they bear the most meaningful fruits of our lives and connect us to true reality. Let's not allow fear, shame, or egos to prevent us from being vulnerable with those we love. It will add value not only to your and their lives, but to society as whole. Carpe Diem!

I am grateful for all the times I've let people be part of my journey. I know I missed out when I didn't by choosing not to be vulnerable. To those who have seen a need to help me, support me, or offer me words of encouragement, you have meaningfully expanded or unstuck my paradigm, giving me personal power—thank you. I am also glad that difficult opportunities arose so I could find the true me. It was not easy, but nothing worthwhile arises from limited effort.

I have been blessed with an amazing and supportive family. To Narciso and Miriam Rodriguez, my parents, who gave up an easier life in the Dominican Republic to create a world of new, amazing opportunities for us in the US, I am eternally grateful for your sacrifice. My siblings, Pedro, Maritza, Rosanna, Aracelis, Rosa, Edwin, and Yahaira—you've given much meaning to my life!

Thank you to those that read my book manuscript and provided comments and suggestions regarding how to make it better. Alan Lesgold, Leighann Sullivan, Cindy Potter, Alexandra Cristiana Georgescu, Corrado Catumaccio, Angela Catumaccio, Andrew Murphy, Rosanna Rodriguez, Edwin Rodriguez, Aisha M. Laspina-Rodriguez, Seth Patel, Peggy Lamb, and Milivel Sardella. My book is a much better product thanks to you and your efforts!

I am grateful to my son, Nathaniel Rodriguez, who coached me on how to make the book more readable to young audiences and was supportive throughout my entire writing journey. I hope I've made you proud!

The amount of support I received during my book-writing journey was unexpected and a great blessing. I am super grateful to the many people who supported my book presale campaign, including Aaron Rudenstine, Adam Minnick, Aida Cruz, Aisha Laspina, Alan Lesgold, Alex Gomez, Alfonso J. Seoage, Alma Mathias, Andrea Zapatka, Andrew Murphy, Ariela Rodriguez, Arturo Conde, Bill Olmo, Brad M. Hutensky, Charo J. Bourdier, Christa Boggio, Corrado Cotumaccio, Craig Robinson, Cristiana Georgescu, Cynthia Potter, Daren Bascome, David Arditi, David Duran, David S.

Ruger, Debora Lehrer, Duggan Jensen, Edwin Rodriguez, Elias Economou, Elias Roman, Elizabeth Lind, Eric Koester, Eric Lora, Eugenio Fernandez, F. James Neil, Jr., Gaurav Kukreja, Jacqueline Dorante, James Gancos, Jay Lee, Jeffrey Eliason, Jeffrey Rutishauser, Jeffrey S. Dvorett, Joe Carrol, John Grogan, Josephine Shum, Joshua Benaim, Josue Sanchez, Juan G. Fernandez, Lance Drucker, Laura Riso, Lee R. Kenna, Les Williams, Lilit Davoyan, Liz Moran, Louis Vintaloro, Luis R. Rodriguez, Luna Gladman, Lynette Guastaferro, Marc Paul Diaz, Maria M. Cruz, Melissa Rodriguez, Milivel Sardella, Mirian Rodriguez, Mitchell A. Cohen, Mostafa Maleki, Nadia Bishai, Narciso Rodriguez, Nathaniel Rodriguez, Olga Votis, Pascual Martinez, Paul Gauthier, Peggy Lamb, Ram Lokan, Regina DiBenedetto, Roberto Rodriguez, Rosanna Rodriguez, Ruby Wei, Satish Shenoy, Shabrina Jiva, Sharmil Modi, Sonja Jackson, Stephen Raff, Susana Quintana-Plaza, Twiggy Alvarez, Wayne Leo, Whitney Heres, William Walsh, and Zack Georgeson, as well as the numerous others who shared my book on social media or helped in other ways. I am honored you have been part of this journey with me. Thank you!

To my business partner and fellow co-founder of Sojourner Glamping, Andrew Murphy, and our colleagues, thank you for being patient with me during this process despite the numerous efforts and deadlines. You are a true friend!

To Melissa, Nathaniel, and Ariela, thank you for your extensive help, support, and patience during this journey. You mean the world to me!

Katherine Mazoyer, Elissa Graeser, and Janie Townsend, thank you for editing and making this a much better book!

And finally, to all those who read this book and pass it on to someone you believe it will help, thank you! I am confident that if enough of us learn how to acknowledge and cultivate our paradigms, we will change the world.

Appendix

———

INTRODUCTION

Eurich, Tasha. "What Self-Awareness Really Is (And How to Cultivate It)." *Harvard Business Review.* January 4, 2018. https://hbr.org/2018/01/what-self-awareness-really-is-and-how-to-cultivate-it.

Eurich, Tasha. "Increase Your Self-Awareness with One Simple Fix." Filmed November 2017 at TedxMileHigh. TED video, 17:17. https://www.ted.com/talks/tasha_eurich_increase_your_self_awareness_wi.

CHAPTER 1

Ariely, Dan. *Predictably Irrational: The Hidden Forces That Shape Our Decisions.* New York, NY: HarperCollins, 2008.

Baron, J. *Thinking and Deciding* (4th ed.). New York, NY: Cambridge University Press, 2007.

Frankfort, H. and H. A., J. A. Wilson, and T. Jacobsen. *Before Philosophy*. Baltimore: Penguin, 1949.

Haselton MG, Nettle D, Andrews PW (2005). "The Evolution of Cognitive Bias." In Buss DM (ed.). *The Handbook of Evolutionary Psychology*. Hoboken, NJ, US: John Wiley & Sons Inc. pp. 724–746.

The Attic. "Helen Keller's Moment." Accessed March 4, 2021. https://www.theattic.space/home-page-blogs/2018/11/29/helen-kellers-moment.

Kahneman D, Tversky A (1972). "Wayback Machine." 2021. Web. Archive.Org. Accessed October 13, 2021. https://web.archive.org/web/20191214120047/http://datacolada.org/wp-content/uploads/2014/08/Kahneman-Tversky-1972.pdf.

Kuhn, Thomas S. *The Structure of Scientific Revolutions*. Chicago: University of Chicago Press, 1970.

Kuhn, Thomas S. *The Structure of Scientific Revolutions*, Chicago: University of Chicago Press (1970, 2nd edition, with postscript).

Nicholson, Nigel. "How Hardwired Is Human Behavior?" *Harvard Business Review*. Accessed October 15, 2021. https://hbr.org/1998/07/how-hardwired-is-human-behavior.

The Decision Lab. "The Illusion of Explanatory Depth." Accessed May 20, 2021. https://thedecisionlab.com/biases/the-illusion-of-explanatory-depth/.

Google Arts & Culture. "The Inspiring Story of Helen Keller." Accessed October 13, 2021. https://artsandculture.google.com/ theme/the-inspiring-story-of-helen-keller/kQJi-1jWXeX_ KQ?hl=en.

Nobelprize.Org. "The Nobel Prize in Physics 1921." Accessed May 20, 2021. https://www.nobelprize.org/prizes/physics

CHAPTER 2

Harari, Yuval N. *Sapiens: A Brief History of Humankind*. New York: Harper, 2015.

Mueller, Paul S., David J. Plevak, and Teresa A. Rummans. 2001. "Religious Involvement, Spirituality, And Medicine: Implications for Clinical Practice." *Mayo Clinic Proceedings* 76 (12): 1225-1235. doi:10.4065/76.12.1225.

Mineo, Liz. "Over Nearly 80 Years, Harvard Study Has Been Showing How to Live a Healthy and Happy Life." *Harvard Gazette*. Accessed August 25, 2021. https://news.harvard.edu/ gazette/story/2017/04/over-nearly-80-years-harvard-study-has-been-showing-how-to-live-a-healthy-and-happy-life/.

Spector, Dina. "The Odds of You Being Alive Are Incredibly Small." *Business Insider*. Accessed September 20, 2021. https:// www.businessinsider.com/infographic-the-odds-of-being-alive-2012-6.

STURM, R. "A Golden Age of Human Pigmentation Genetics." *Trends In Genetics* 22. 2006. (9): 464-468. doi:10.1016/j. tig.2006.06.010.

Harvard Business School. "Warren Buffett Speaks At HBS."
Accessed September 20, 2021. https://www.alumni.hbs.edu/
stories/Pages/story-bulletin.aspx?num=2406.

CHAPTER 3

Alter, Charlotte, Suyin Haynes, and Justin Worland. "Time 2019
Person of the Year—Greta Thunberg." *Time.com*. Accessed
September 23, 2021. https://time.com/person-of-the-year-2019-
greta-thunberg/.

Britton, Bianca. "Greta Thunberg Labeled A 'Brat' By Brazilian
President Jair Bolsonaro." *CNN*. Accessed April 20, 2021.
https://www.cnn.com/2019/12/11/americas/bolsonaro-thun-
berg-brat-intl-scli/index.html.

Brown, Brené. "The Power of Vulnerability." Filmed June 2010 at
TEDxHouston. TED video, 20:03. https://www.ted.com/talks/
Brené_brown_th.

Burgess, Sanya. "Margaret Atwood Says Greta Thunberg Is The
'Joan of Arc of The Environment'." *Sky News*. Accessed April 20,
2021. https://news.sky.com/story/margaret-atwood-says-gre-
ta-thunberg-is-the-joan-of-arc-of-the-environment-11855734.

Green, Matthew and Valerie Volovici. "'How Dare You': Greta
Thunberg Gives Powerful, Emotional Speech to the UN—
National | Globalnews.Ca." *Global News*. Accessed April
20, 2021. https://globalnews.ca/news/5940258/greta-thun-
berg-speech-un/.

Rowlatt, Justin. "Greta Thunberg, The Climate Campaigner Who Doesn't Like Campaigning." *BBC News*. Accessed April 20, 2021. https://www.bbc.com/news/stories-53255535.

Rourke, Alison. "Greta Thunberg Responds to Asperger's Critics: 'It's A Superpower'." *The Guardian*. Accessed April 20, 2021. https://www.theguardian.com/environment/2019/sep/02/greta-thunberg-responds-to-aspergers-critics-its-a-superpower.

Democracy Now! "School Strike for Climate: Meet 15-Year-Old Activist Greta Thunberg, Who Inspired a Global Movement." Accessed April 20, 2021. https://www.democracynow.org/2018/12/1.

Sutter, John and Lawrence Davidson. CNN. 2018. "Teen Tells Climate Negotiators They Aren't Mature Enough." *CNN*. Accessed April 20, 2021. https://www.cnn.com/2018/12/16/world/greta-thunberg-cop24/index.html.

Thunberg, Greta. 2021. "The Disarming Case to Act Right Now on Climate Change." Filmed November 2018 at TEDxStockholm. TED video, 11:03 https://www.ted.com/talks/greta_thunberg.

CHAPTER 4

Adams, Tim. "John Cacioppo: 'Loneliness Is Like an Iceberg—It Goes Deeper Than We Can See.'" *The Guardian*. February 28, 2016.

Brown, Brené. "The Power of Vulnerability." Filmed June 2010 at TEDxHouston. TED video, 20:03. https://www.ted.com/talks/Brené_brown_th.

Cacioppo, John. "Loneliness Is Like an Iceberg—It Goes Deeper Than We Can See." *The Guardian.* Accessed August 25, 2021. https://www.theguardian.com/science/2016/feb/28/loneliness-is-like-an-iceberg-john-cacioppo-social-neuroscience-interview.

Karma, Roge. "Former Surgeon General Vivek Murthy on America's Loneliness Epidemic." *Vox.* Accessed September 10, 2021. https://www.vox.com/2020/5/11/21245087/america-loneliness-epidemic-coronavirus-pandemic-together.

Murthy, Vivek. *Together.* New York, NY: HarperCollins, 2020.

Sweet, Jacob. "The Loneliness Pandemic." *Harvard Magazine.* Accessed September 10, 2021. https://www.harvardmagazine.com/2021/01/feature-the-loneliness-pandemic.

Thomas Kuhn. "What Are Scientific Revolutions?" An excerpt from The Probabilistic Revolution, Volume I: Ideas in History, eds. Lorenz Kruger, Lorraine, J. Daston, and Michael Heidelberger (Cambridge, MA: MIT Press, 1987), pp. 7-22.

HHS.Gov. "Vice Admiral Vivek H. Murthy, MD, MBA." Accessed August 20, 2021. https://www.hhs.gov/about/leadership/vivek-murthy.html.

CHAPTER 5

Harvard Business School. "About–Harvard Business School." Accessed 13 September 2021. https://www.hbs.edu/about/Pages/default.aspx.

Northjersey.com. "Inside the Journey that Brought Bergen County's Shane Griffith a NCAA Wrestling Title." Accessed 11 September 2021. https://www.northjersey.com/story/sports/college/wrestling/2021/04/06/keep-stanford-wrestling-inside-shane-griffiths-road-ncaa-title/7104712002/.

Bonagura, Kyle. "Stanford Reconsiders, Won't Eliminate 11 Sports." May 18,2021. *ESPN.Com.* Accessed 12 September 2021. https://www.espn.com/college-sports/story/_/id/31467258/with-new-optimism-based-new-circumstances-stanford-reverses-controversial-decision-eliminate-11-varsity-sports.

Bumbaca, Chris. "Shane Griffith Uses NCAA Championship to Highlight 'Keep Stanford Wrestling' Efforts." March 22, 2021. *USA Today.* Accessed 12 September 2021. https://www.usatoday.com/story/sports/college/2021/03/22/shane-griffith-ncaa-title-keep-stanford-wrestling/4799900001/.

Chernow, Ron. *Alexander Hamilton.* London: Penguin Books, 2004.

Delman, Edward. "How Lin-Manuel Miranda Shapes History." *The Atlantic.* Retrieved July 11, 2021. https://www.theatlantic.com/entertainment/archive/2015/09/lin-manuel-miranda-hamilton/408019/.

Encyclopedia Britannica Online. Academic ed. s.v. "Founding Fathers—The Explanations." Accessed 10 May 2021. https://www.britannica.com/topic/Founding-Fathers/The-explanations.

Encyclopedia Britannica Online. Academic ed. s.v. "Learned Help-lessness: Description, History, & Applications." Accessed September 13, 2021. https://www.britannica.com/science/learned-helplessness.

Falk, Steven. "Shane Griffith Enables Stanford Wrestling Program to Go Out On Top With NCAA Tournament Title." *Asbury Park Press.* Accessed 12 September 2021. https://www.app.com/story/sports/college/2021/03/20/shane-griffith-enables-stanford-wrestling-program-go-out-top/4780172001/.

Gioia, Michael. "History in the Making—Revolutionary Musical 'Hamilton' Opens on Broadway Tonight." *Playbill.* Accessed October 14, 2021.

Paulson, Michael. "'Hamilton' Makes History with 16 Tony Nominations (Published 2016)". 2016. *Nytimes.Com.* Accessed October 14, 2021. https://www.nytimes.com/2016/05/04/theater/hamilton-tony-nominations-record.html.

Keepstanfordwrestling.Com. "Keep Stanford Wrestling." Accessed 12 September 2021. https://www.keepstanfordwrestling.com/.

Morehead, James. "Stanford University's Carol Dweck on The Growth Mindset and Education." *Onedublin.Org.* Accessed 13 September 2021. https://onedublin.org/2012/06/19/stanford-universitys-carol-dweck-on-the-growth-mindset-and-education/.

"Patriotism on Broadway". 2015. *The Economist.* Accessed October 14, 2021. https://www.economist.com/books-and-arts/2015/12/16/patriotism-on-broadway.

Paulson, Michael. "In The Heights: 'Hamilton' Reaches Top Tier at Broadway Box Office." *Artsbeat.* Accessed October 14, 2021. https://artsbeat.blogs.nytimes.com/2015/09/08/hamilton-with-higher-prices-would-make-a-treasury-secretary-proud/.

Rooney, David. "'Hamilton' Wins 2016 Pulitzer Prize for Drama— The Hollywood Reporter." April 18, 2016. *Hollywood Reporter.* https://www.hollywoodreporter.com/lifestyle/arts/hamilton-wins-2016-pulitzer-prize-884618/.

Scekic, Sofia. "Wrestler Shane Griffith Named Rookie of The Year | The Stanford Daily." May 30, 2020. *The Stanford Daily.* Accessed September 12, 2021. https://www.stanforddaily.com/2020/05/30/wrestler-shane-griffith-named-rookie-of-the-year/.

Seligman, Martin E.P. "Building Resilience." *Harvard Business Review.* Accessed 13 September 2021] https://hbr.org/2011/04/building-resilience.

CHAPTER 6

Argyris, Chris. "Teaching Smart People How to Learn" (PDF). *Harvard Business Review.* 69 (3): 99–109. Retrieved 14 September 2021.

Cartwright, Shannon. "Double-Loop Learning: A Concept and Process For Leadership Educators—Journal Of Leadership Education." *Journal Of Leadership Education.* Accessed 14 September 2021. https://journalofleadershiped.org/jole_articles/double-loop-learning-a-concept-and-process-for-leadership-educators/.

Marra, Marci. "The Power of Your Words." *Thriveglobal.Com.* Accessed 14 September 2021. https://thriveglobal.com/stories/the-power-of-your-words-2/.

Turkle, Sherry. *Reclaiming Conversation: The Power of Talk in a Digital Age.* Penguin Press, 2015.

Ury, William. "The Power of Listening." Filmed October 2010 at TEDxSanDiego. TED video, 18:29. Accessed 14 September 2021. https://www.tedxsandiego.com/transcripts/2014-talks/william-ury/.

Weir, Peter. *Dead Poets Society.* Buena Vista Pictures Distribution, 1989.

CHAPTER 7

Barrett, Lisa. 2021. "You Aren't at the Mercy of Your Emotions—Your Brain Creates Them." Filmed December 2017 at TED@IBM. TED video, 18:20. Accessed 10 September 2021. https://www.ted.com/talks/lisa_feldman_barrett_you_aren_t_at_the_mercy_of_your_emotions_your_brain_creates_them?language=en.

Barrett, L. F. *How Emotions Are Made: The Secret Life of the Brain.* New York City: Houghton Mifflin Harcourt, 2017.

Kingjamesbibleonline.org. "JOHN 8:4 KJV: They Say unto Him, Master, This Woman Was Taken in Adultery, in the Very Act." Accessed 14 September, 2021. https://www.kingjamesbibleonline.org/John-8-4/.

Medrut, Flavia. "25 Beautiful Robert Frost Quotes on Life and Human Nature." 2019. *Goalcast*. Accessed September 25, 2021. https://www.goalcast.com/robert-frost-quotes/.

Merriam-Webster Online. 11th ed. s.v. "Complaining." Accessed 31 May 2021. https://www.merriam-webster.com/diction ary/complaining.

Myers, DG. *Psychology* (Seventh Edition). New York, NY: Worth Publishers, 2004.

Schwantes, Marcel. "How To Instantly Improve Work Communication by Zapping This Toxic Habit." November 30, 2016. *Inc.Com*. Accessed 13 September 2021. https://www.inc.com/marcel-schwantes/how-to-instantly-improve-work-communication-by-zapping-this-toxic-habit.html.

Senge, Peter M. *The Fifth Discipline: The Art & Practice of the Learning Organization*. New York City: Currency Publishing, 2006.

CHAPTER 8

Allen, T., 2021. *This Is What It Takes to Become a Successful Management Consultant*. Forbes. Accessed 13 June 2021. https://www.forbes.com/sites/terinaallen/2020/02/26/this-is-what-it-takes-to-become-a-successful-management-consultant/?sh=72ce2d-8f4ce1.

April, Kurt A, Babar Dharani, Kai Peters. "Impact of Locus of Control Expectancy on Level of Well-Being." Review of European Studies. 4 (2). Accessed 14 August 2021. doi:10.5539/res.v4n2p124.

Bandura, Albert (1971). "Social Learning Theory." (PDF) General Learning Corporation. Archived from the original (PDF) on 24 October 2013. "Wayback Machine." Web.Archive.org. Accessed 3 September 2021. https://web.archive.org/web/20131024214.

Christensen, Clayton. "Biography." Accessed 12 June 2021. https://claytonchristensen.com/biography/.

Christensen, Clay. *How Will You Measure Your Life?* Harper Collins: New York, 2012.

Eurich, Tasha. 2017. "Transcript Of 'Increase Your Self-Awareness with One Simple Fix.'" *Ted.com.* Accessed 14 August 2021. https://www.ted.com/talks/tasha_eurich_increase_your_self_awareness_with_one_simple_fix/transcript?language=en.

Fandom.com: *Shawshank Redemption Wiki.* Accessed 14 September 2021. https://shawshank.fandom.com/wiki/The_Shawshank_Redemption#:~:text=Chicago%20Sun%2DTimes%20film%20reviewer,placed%20in%20a%20hopeless%20position.

University of Virginia. 2021. *Faculty.Darden.Virginia.Edu.* Accessed 14 August 2021. https://faculty.darden.virginia.edu/clawsonj/General/SELF_ASSESSMENT_TOOLS/OB-786_Locus_of_Control.pdf.

CHAPTER 9

Brown, Judith M. *Gandhi: Prisoner of Hope.* New Haven: Yale University Press, 1989.

Dhiman, Satinder. *Gandhi And Leadership*. New York: Palgrave Macmillan US, 2015.

Gandhi, Mahatma, Leo Tolstoy, and B. Srinivasa Murthy. *Mahatma Gandhi and Leo Tolstoy Letters*. Long Beach, Calif.: Long Beach Publications, 1987.

George, Bill, Diana Mayer, Andrew N. McLean, and Peter Sims. "Discovering Your Authentic Leadership." 2007. *Harvard Business Review*. Accessed October 1, 2021. https://hbr.org/2007/02/discovering-your-authentic-leadership.

Gandhi, Mohandas K. *An Autobiography, or, The Story of My Experiments With Truth*. London: Penguin, 2007.

Guha, Ramchandra. *Gandhi before India*. New York City: Vintage Books, 2015.

Herman, Arthur. *Gandhi & Churchill*. New York: Bantam Books, 2008.

Maeleine Slade, Mirabehn. *Gleanings Gathered at Bapu's Feet*. Ahmedabad: Navjivan Publications, 1949.

Rai, Ajay Shanker. *Gandhian Satyagraha*. New Delhi: Concept Publ. Comp., 2000.

Sharma, Arvind. (2013). *Gandhi: A Spiritual Biography*. New Haven: Yale University Press, 2013.

McHugh, Caroline. "The Art of Being Yourself." Filmed at TEDxMiltonKEynesWomen. TED Video, 26:23. https://www.

thecolourworks.com/ted-talk-caroline-mchugh-the-art-of-being-yourself/.

Toffin, Gerard. John Zavos; et al. (eds.). *Public Hinduisms*. Thousand Oaks, CA: Sage Publications. 2012.

Vahed, Goolem and Ashwin Desai. *South African Gandhi—Stretcher-Bearer of Empire*. Stanford: Stanford University Press, 2015.

Weber, Thomas. *Gandhi As Disciple and Mentor*. Cambridge: Cambridge University Press, 2011.

Harvard Business School. "William W. George—Faculty & Research—Harvard Business School." Accessed October 2, 2021. https://www.hbs.edu/faculty/Pages/profile.aspx?-facId=275677.

CHAPTER 10

"A Quote By Ernest Hemingway/" *Goodreads.com*. Accessed October 2, 2021. https://www.goodreads.com/quotes/1501875-we-are-all-broken-that-s-how-the-light-gets-in.

Filkins, Peter. "Words Preserved Against a Day of Fear—The American Scholar." *The American Scholar*. Accessed October 2, 2021. https://theamericanscholar.org/words-preserved-against-a-day-of-fear/.

Imdb.om. "The Great Debaters." Accessed October 2, 2021. https://www.imdb.com/title/tt0427309/.

Twitter.com "Manson, Mark Quote of July 13, 2020." Accessed October 2, 2021. https://twitter.com/StephenRCovey/status/1282642255044640773.

Mineo, Liz. "Good Genes are Nice, but Joy is Better." *Harvard Gazette.* Accessed October 2, 2021. https://news.harvard.edu/gazette/story/2017/04/over-nearly-80-years-harvard-study-has-been-showing-how-to-live-a-healthy-and-happy-life/.

"People Will Do Anything, No Matter How Absurd, To Avoid Facing Their Own Soul.—Carl Jung—School of Practical Philosophy Australia." *School Of Practical Philosophy Australia.* Accessed October 2, 2021. https://practicalphilosophy.org.au/people-will-do-anything-no-matter-how-absurd-to-avoid-facing-their-own-soul-carl-jung/.

Soltes, Eugene. n.d. *Why They Do It.* New York: Public Affairs, 2016.

Sparks, William. "The Power of Self-Awareness." Filmed September 2018 at TedxAshville. Ted Video, 18:09. Accessed October 2, 2021. https://www.ted.com/talks/william_l_spark.

McHugh, Caroline. "The Art of Being Yourself." Filmed at TEDxMiltonKEynesWomen. TED Video, 26:23. https://www.thecolourworks.com/ted-talk-caroline-mchugh-the-art-of-being-yourself/.

University of Texas. "Behavioral Ethics—Ethics Unwrapped." *Ethics Unwrapped.* Accessed October 2, 2021. https://ethicsunwrapped.utexas.edu/subject-area/behavioral-ethics.

Washington, Denzel. *The Great Debaters*. 2007. United States: Metro-Goldwyn-Mayer.

"What Should I Read." Accessed October 2, 2021. https://www.whatshouldireadnext.com/quotes/atticus-poetry-we-are-all-born-free.

CHAPTER 11

Elkins, Kathleen. "Warren Buffett Says the Most Important Decision You'll Ever Make Has Nothing to Do with Your Money or Career." *CNBC*. Accessed October 5, 2021. https://www.cnbc.com/2018/05/14/warren-buffett-says-the-most-important-decision-is-who-you-marry.html.

Expanded Books. "Daniel Goleman—Social Intelligence." September 25, 2006. Video, 4:11. https://www.youtube.com/watch?v=nZskNGdP_zM.

Goleman, Daniel. "About Daniel Goleman—Daniel Goleman." Accessed August 20, 2021. *Danielgoleman.Info*. https://www.danielgoleman.info/biography.

Ito, Tiffany, and Jennifer Kubota. "Social Neuroscience." *Noba*. Accessed October 5, 2021. https://nobaproject.com/modules/social-neuroscience#abstract.

Pirnia, Garin. "13 Facts About Cast Away." *Mentalfloss*. Accessed October 5, 2021. https://www.mentalfloss.com/article/72907/13-surprising-facts-about-cast-away.

PsychAlive. "Dr. Dan Siegel—'What is Mindsight?'" December 17, 2009. Video, 2:11. https://www.youtube.com/watch?v=IK-wQuGCPeFk.

Siegel, Dan. "Biography—Dr. Dan Siegel." *Dr. Dan Siegel.* 2021. https://drdansiegel.com/biography/.

CHAPTER 12

"Adolf Hitler | Biography, Rise to Power, & Facts." *Encyclopedia Britannica.* Accessed 25 June 2021. https://www.britannica.com/biography/Adolf-Hitler.

Bullock, Alan. *Hitler: A Study in Tyranny.* London: Penguin Books. 1962.

Hamann, Brigitte. *Hitler's Vienna: A Portrait of the Tyrant as a Young Man.* Trans. Thomas Thornton. London; New York: Tauris Parke Paperbacks, 1999/2010.

Hayes, Britt. "See the Cast of 'School Ties' Then and Now." *Screencrush.* Accessed July 10, 2021. https://screencrush.com/see-the-cast-of-school-ties-then-and-now/#:~:text=Based%20on%20the%20real%2Dlife,background%20from%20his%20antisemitic%20classmates.

Hitler, Adolf. *Mein Kampf.* Trans. Ralph Manheim. Boston: Houghton Mifflin, 1999/ 1925.

Kershaw, Ian. *Hitler: A Biography.* New York: W. W. Norton & Company, 2008.

Kershaw, Ian. *Hitler: 1889–1936: Hubris.* New York: W. W. Norton & Company, 1999.

CHAPTER 13

Friedman, Ron. "Regular Exercise Is Part of Your Job." *Harvard Business Review.* October 3, 2014. https://hbr.org/2014/10/regular-exercise-is-part-of-your-job.

Selhub, Eva. "Nutritional Psychiatry: Your Brain on Food—Harvard Health." *Harvard Health.* March 26, 2020, https://www.health.harvard.edu/blog/nutritional-psychiatry-your-brain-on-food-201511168626.

Scharper, Julie. "Lighten Up—According to Science, It's Good for You." *The Hub.* Accessed 23 June 2021. https://hub.jhu.edu/magazine/2016/summer/neuroscience-of-fun/.

Troxel, Wendy M. "Want to Keep Your Relationship on Solid Ground? Get Enough Sleep." *Ideas.Ted.Com,* 2021. Accessed 23 June 2021. https://ideas.ted.com/want-to-keep-your-relationship-on-solid-ground-get-enough-sleep/..